THE FASCISTI EXPOSED

GIACOMO MATTEOTTI

THE
FASCISTI EXPOSED

A YEAR OF
FASCIST DOMINATION

By

GIACOMO MATTEOTTI

Translated by
E. W. DICKES

HOWARD FERTIG

New York · 1969

First published in English in 1924

HOWARD FERTIG, INC. EDITION 1969

Library of Congress Catalog Card Number: 68-9637

PRINTED IN THE UNITED STATES OF AMERICA
BY NOBLE OFFSET PRINTERS, INC.

CONTENTS.

INTRODUCTION

On the 10th of June, 1924, a man was kidnapped in one of the streets of Rome, taken away in a car and cruelly murdered. Two months later dogs found his martyred body with a rasp still sticking in his pierced breast. It was Giacomo Matteotti, the secretary of the Italian Socialist Party and the intellectual leader of the Opposition in the Italian Parliament.

There is no better test of a man's life than his death. And there is no truer evidence of how the victim fell than that given by one of his murderers, who confessed that Matteotti's last words were :—"You may kill me; you will not kill the ideal. My children will be proud of their father. The workers will bless my dead body." These words, reported by one of his torturers, could not have been invented.

Giacomo Matteotti died at the age of 39. He was brought up in comfortable surroundings and given an extensive education which made him acquainted with foreign languages (especially English, which he acquired at Oxford) and foreign studies. He easily found access to a brilliant career in juridical science. This he gave up, however, in order to take his place in the ranks of his party—the party of freedom and justice of a higher degree than that afforded by present laws. Came the war. Matteotti stood against it, and, as a fighter against fighting, he was imprisoned for years in a dungeon in Sicily. After the war he gradually rose to prominence. Unlike most of his countrymen he was a man of cool, intellectual judgment, controlling a fiery heart and a firm will. He was aware of his nation's emotional boundlessness and tried to avoid it. He was a man of fact, a teacher as well as a leader to his followers. He taught them prudence and held them back from risky adventures while never hesitating to dare himself.

The last time he left his native country, just a few weeks before he fell, he was refused a passport and crossed the frontier in disguise. But he returned to Italy undisguised and himself disclosed his identity to the authorities. We asked him why he should run such a risk and he answered simply :—"Our people want encouragement. They will see that one need not put up with everything."

I remember another word he spoke during his short stay in this country. He was speaking of the sufferings of his fellow-workers in Italy. "The worst," said he, "what even the strongest amongst our people cannot stand is that, for the last two years, when a man leaves his home in the morning he does not know whether he will return that night . . ." He said it very quietly. And he went back—to die. He died because he had spoken to the world of what the Italian people are going through and because he was going to say more. After his great speech in the Chamber, in which he vigorously denounced the violence and mockery of the so-called "elections" in Italy—a speech which enraged the artificial majority, the products and puppets of this election—the official Press hinted at him, threatening that he would have to be "silenced." Soon it appeared that his murder had been plotted and executed by a gang of criminals composed of some of the highest officials of the Fascist Government and party and most intimate friends and counsellors of Mussolini himself. And, though contemporary history scribblers are busy white-washing the Dictator's person from the stains of this blood, there is something to be said about the responsibility in an autocratic system which focuses all power upon one person. Fascism has always boasted of having done away with democracy and its system of responsibilities and has always proclaimed the identity of party and government. It is not Fascism which could to-day disclaim the culpability of the whole system when criminals rank amongst its most respected servants. It cannot term them outcasts to-day when they have been instruments until yesterday.

There is yet another word to be added. But for the

chance that a witness noted the number of the car in which Matteotti was abducted there would have been no clue and he would simply have disappeared—like so many others. We know to-day that a number of persons witnessed what happened in a street of the capital and yet did not venture to intervene, having become accustomed to similar displays by the ruling power. Can we say more in condemnation of the type of order actually in force in Italy? Need we say more to prove that Matteotti is but one of hundreds, perhaps thousands, who died like him—unknown fighters for freedom and victims of violence?

Let him say it himself. In this book, which he was forced to publish anonymously, he has recorded the deeds of Fascism during the first year of its reign. He was about to add the chronicle of the second year. He was not allowed to finish. He had to prove by his death that what he has registered with almost striking sobriety in these pages, which we read to-day with profound emotion, is, in fact, true to the very letter. Suddenly that letter has turned red. Never was it more cruelly true to say that a man has written with his heart's blood.

And never has another word become more true than those prophetic words of the dying hero—they killed him but they were unable to kill the ideal for which he stood. They tried to stop a fighting force, and they have stirred a whole nation. They wanted to silence a single man, and they have raised a world-wide movement of horror and protest. They killed one, and there are hundreds eager to take his place in the ranks. They stabbed Matteotti to death, and he is still alive; they buried his body, and his spirit is amongst us, leading and fighting more than ever.

OSKAR POLLAK.

September, 1924.

THE FASCISTI EXPOSED.

A YEAR OF FASCIST DOMINATION.

The Fascist Government justifies its armed conquest of political power, its use of violence and the risk it incurred of igniting civil war, by the plea of the urgent necessity of restoring the authority of law and the State, and of rescuing the country from economic and financial conditions approaching utter ruin.

The statistical and historical data and documents compiled in this book are a demonstration of the very contrary of this. They show that never as in this last year, during which Fascism has been in power, has the law been so thrust aside in favour of arbitrary action, the State so subjugated by a faction, or the nation so split up into two classes, a dominating and a subject class. The country's economic and financial condition has, on the whole, continued to show the improvement and the slow recovery from the devastation of the war, which had already begun in the preceding years; but had begun thanks to the energies of the people, not the excesses and extravagances of Fascist domination. As to this latter, one thing is demonstrably true : that the profits of the speculators and the capitalists have increased in proportion as the reward of labour and the small resources of the middle classes have diminished, while these two latter classes have lost all freedom and all that is of worth in citizenship.

PART I.

THE ECONOMIC AND FINANCIAL SITUATION.

1. *The Exchange.* The first promise made to the country by the new rulers was to restore the Italian lira in a short time to the value of 50 gold centesimi.[1] The promise was a manifestation of the Fascists' faith in miracles. While they were preaching the liberation of things economic from State control, they were dreaming of exerting by political measures an immediate influence upon things economic. In point of fact, the tendency of the Italian lira to stabilisation and slow improvement had already been manifested before the coming of Fascism to power, and if the international questions arising out of the war could have been settled the improvement would have been still more rapid.

In 1919-20 the agreement with the Allies which artificially pegged the exchange came to an end; and the exchange fell precipitously, revealing all the damage done by the war. In 1921 and 1922 there were various oscillations, with a tendency towards stabilisation and improvement. In 1923, that is the year of Fascist rule, the exchange has tended rather to *worsen* than the contrary, in comparison with 1922. The average rate at which the dollar was quoted in the Italian exchanges during January to September, 1922, was 20.9 lire; during 1923, the Fascist year, 21.7 lire.

2. *The Balance of Trade.* The war had gravely affected the balance of foreign trade, but from 1920 onwards there was a steady movement in the direction of a return to pre-war conditions—once more with no aid from miracle-workers. (It should be mentioned that after June, 1921, there was a change in the method of valuation, tending to reduce the figures.)

---

[1] That is, to half of its pre-war value, instead of about one-quarter.—*Trans.*

			Imports.	Exports.	Deficit.
			(in millions of lire.)		
First six months	1914	...	1.888	1.285	603
,,	,,	1920	...	14.007	5.985	8.022
,,	,,	1921	...	8.749	3.962	4.787
,,	,,	1922	...	7.772	4.200	3.572
,,`	,,	1923	...	9.073	4.886	4.187
July to September,	1922	...	3.417	2.150	1.267
,,	,,	1923	...	3.616	2.440	1.176
Year 1913	...	...	...	3.667	2.592	1.075
,, 1920	...	...	...	26.840	11.775	15.065
,, 1921	...	...	...	17.238	8.277	8.961
,, 1922	...	...	...	15.770	9.297	6.473

Despite the deficit in the balance of trade, the balance of foreign debts and credits could be regarded as already in Italy's favour from the beginning of 1922 onwards, that is under the old regime. Professor Iannacone's figures for 1922 were as follows:

Debtor balances	...	7,518 millions
Credit balances	...	7,746 millions
Surplus	... ...	228 millions

3. *Note circulation, reserves, and advances.* Official or semi-official communications of the Fascist press have announced that "The circulation has been reduced to a notable extent. At the entry into power of the Fascist Government, it exceeded 18 milliards of lire; now it is about 16 milliards" (Gangemi, of the Ministerial Press Bureau, in the *Europe Nouvelle,* "L'Italie de Mussolini"), "reducing it by more than 2 milliards, or 300 millions a month, while the preceding Governments took nearly two years to reduce it by 1½ milliards." (Communication of the Volta news agency, June 21, 1923.)

The truth, as is shown by the documents, is as follows. The circulation reached its maximum in December, 1920, owing to the last of the extraordinary expenditure due to the war and of the special estimates for victualling, which were *brought to an end* by the Giolitti Government in the winter of 1921. Recovery began in 1921, and would have reached two milliards but for the crash of the Banca di Sconto, which brought the circulation over 19 milliards. In 1922 the improvement recommenced, and reached *nearly* 1½ *milliards*. On the other hand, 1923, the Fascist year, shows month by month figures which average *less than a milliard* below the corresponding months of 1922, and in June, July and August *less than half a milliard*.

Thus there continues, fortunately, the slight tendency to improve which already characterised the preceding years ; but, once more, in this field the new Government has produced no miracle.

		Millions [1]
December, 1920		19.732
January to June, 1921 ...		18.560
July to November, 1921 ...		17.940
December, 1921		19.209

		1922	1923
January		18.755	17.466
February		18.258	17.153
March		18.113	17.035
April		17.711	16.685
May		17.320	16,280
June		17.823	17.337
July		17.997	17.382
August		17.747	17.035
September ...		17.989	17.145
October			17.238

} 261 [2]

[1] The figures include the whole of the Italian paper circulation with the exception of the State notes for 5 and 10 lire and the *buoni di cassa,* which have remained unaltered.

[2] From May, 1923, onwards, the official figures do not include the amount of the 25 lira notes, namely, 261 million lire, which

The reserves were as follows:

Year	Gold Millions	Silver Millions	Foreign securities or deposits Millions
1920	1,059	115	903
1921	1,092	114	792
1922	1,126	116	799
1923	1,134	116	603

The advances made by note issuing institutions have decreased as shown by the following table, once more without any remarkable change:

	Millions
December, 1921	4,839
January to April, 1922 ...	4,167
May to June, 1922	3,622
July to October, 1922 ...	3,068
July to October, 1923 ...	2,972

4. *Deposits; savings; postal, telegraph, and telephone revenues; pawnshops.*

The total savings were:

		Millions
June 30, 1920		20,659
,, 1921		26,618
,, 1922		28,316
,, 1923		32,334

—that is, an increase in 1923 equivalent to the average of preceding years.

The revenue of the Ministry of Posts and Telegraphs was as follows:

		Millions
1919-20		344
1920-21		509
1921-22		632

were transferred under the decree of April 26th, 1923, from the banknote circulation to that of the State, which actually increased from 1,867 millions in 1922 to 2,028 millions in 1923. The transfer is one of accounting only, and the sum of 261 millions must therefore be added for exactitude in comparison.

First six months, Millions.

1922	...	...	...	...	585
1923	...	...	...	...	623

—that is, an average increase, with no notable change.

The pledges taken by the pawnshops, however, continued to increase:

January, 1921	...	75,235
,, 1922	...	152,306
,, 1923	...	179,568
September, 1923	...	204,437

5. *Prices, bankruptcies, share capital.* In 1923, the prices of commodities increased on the average. It is not desired to hold the Fascist party responsible for this; but the fact may serve to disillusion those who threw all the blame for the rising prices of former years upon the workers. Wholesale prices (Bachi index) averaged 696 in 1922 and 726 in 1923.

Owing to the decrees removing restrictions upon rents, the rents of dwellings, an important part of the cost of living, *increased* on the average 40 to 50 per cent., and will continue to increase, while reduced consumption may perhaps bring reductions of prices.

There has been a great increase in the average monthly number of bankruptcies:

Monthly average

1920	...	...	...	52
1921	...	...	...	149
1922	...	...	...	297
1923 (nine months' average)				443

The share capital investments have increased:

Monthly average — Million lire

1920	...	...	...	423
1921	...	...	...	288
1922	...	...	...	232
1923 (nine months' average)				383

6. *Profits and Wages.* Stock exchange industrial quotations improved, acording to the Bachi index, from a minimum of 56.45 in April, 1922, to 67.47 in September (under the old regime). Under the Fascist regime the figures are

October, 1922	...	70.16
January, 1923	...	72.93
July	...	76.62
August ...	...	80.49

Italian consols improved as follows:

January, 1922	...	75.9
September ...	...	81.8
January, 1923	...	84.4
September ...	...	88.3
October ...	...	89.2

Wages have, on the contrary, greatly *diminished.* The average in the metal and engineering industries was about 25 lire a day in 1921 and 19 in 1923, or a diminution *exceeding* 20 *per cent.* In the textile, building, chemical, etc., industries the reduction is also estimated at 10 to 20 per cent., even 30 per cent. in the small centres. Only in certain small industries and in printing is the reduction less than 10 per cent.

In agriculture the average of the reductions effected by the pacts imposed by the Fascist groups or the farmers, as compared with the pacts formerly freely concluded between the employers' and workers' confederations, is about 10 to 15 per cent. in actual wages; but the effective reduction is brought above 20 per cent. by the lapse or restriction of the former guarantees of employment, the altered terms for other than normal work, and so on.

According to the figures compiled by the National Accident Insurance Bureau, the general average of daily wages has diminished from 18.74 lire in 1921 to 17.05

in 1923, that is *ten per cent*. In the most important industrial centres the reduction is greater :

Turin, from 18.97 to 16.54 lire.
Milan, from 17.80 to 16.17 lire.
Genoa, from 22.80 to 20.28 lire.
Bologna, from 19.00 to 16.56 lire.

—that is *thirteen per cent.*

If, then, the national economic indices show that the slow and painful reconstruction following the damage of the war still continues ; if the indices of capitalist profits are increasing ; and if only wages are decidedly diminishing ; the conclusion is that the existing regime has brought no extraordinary improvement in economic conditions in the country as a whole, but has made only this innovation—that economic recovery is continuing, *but at the exclusive cost of the poorer classes.*

7. *Unemployment, emigration, strikes.* Official statistics record a marked diminution of industrial unemployment.

Monthly average
1920	...	...	....	143,833
1921	...	...	...	445,000
1922	...	...	...	409,390
1923 (eight months' average)				261,494

But the statistics lack uniformity and are *hardly worth attention.*

In 1920-21 the statistical returns were entrusted to the Communes, and were made the basis of the grant of assistance and of relief works. It was thus evidently to the interest of the compiling authorities to swell the figures, which were not methodically collected. Now the data are collected in the Prefectures by Government commissioners, who work on restrictive lines, demanding personal report and a severe test which, especially in the rural districts, ends apparently in eliminating from the returns an important part of the unemployment which actually exists.

A correct estimate, however, of economic conditions requires count to be taken of the Italians who, failing to find employment in their own country, have sought it abroad. The Italian emigration registered in 1921-22 amounted to 180,000; the actual figure was probably about 225,000, which after deducting 80,000 repatriated leaves a net emigration figure of 145,000. The official figure for 1922-23 was 309,000, the actual probably 400,000, and repatriation 60,000, leaving net emigration 340,000. Adding this to the 261,000 unemployed, we have a total substantially in excess of the corresponding figures for preceding years.

The Fascists have made much of the fact that there have been fewer strikes: 156 during the first Fascist year, 680 in the year before, with a reduction of 90 per cent. in the number of strikers.

There is no doubt that the bludgeon and the absolute non-existence of freedom of organisation and assembly are a material hindrance to strikes. A century ago there were no strikes at all. To-day in Italy no men strike or can strike except *the members of the Fascist organisations.*

But the numbers of strikes are also influenced by economic conditions. In periods of crisis and economic depression the number of strikes diminishes. The British experience shows this. There, there is neither Bolshevism nor Fascism, and despite full liberty the number of strikers in 1921 was 1,801,000, with 85 million days lost, and in 1923 (nine months) 358,000, with eight million days lost.

Note.—The Ministry of Agriculture and the Fascist papers have taken credit for the increased grain crop of 1922-23, which amounted to 54 million quintals, showing an excess over 1921-22. But the crop was sown under the old regime; the variations of crops are mainly dependent on the season and the rains; and if politics are to be brought in, the crop of the Bolshevist year 1920-21 was 52½ million quintals or almost as much as the Fascists' crop!

Fascism has even claimed credit for the increase in the traffic of the port of Genoa. But (a) the traffic increased 13 per cent. in 1922 as compared with 1921; (b) the increase in 1923, the Fascist year, was mainly due to arrivals of British coal, through the falling off of reparation coal from the Ruhr, and to increased imports of grain to make good the poor harvest of 1922. And, on the other hand, the taxes of Genoa have been increased. For instance, the tax on lighters has been increased from 5-20 to 30-100 lire. And the decree of September 15, 1923, has imposed the following fresh taxes: an additional 5 centesimi per ton on arrivals, with a further 5 centesimi for anchorage; 50 lire per metric ton taken in or discharged; 2 lire per railway wagon; 1 to 40 lire for every passenger. There is a charge of 2,400,000 lire per annum for the Fascist Militia now policing the port, and virtually employed on purely political duties. There has been a certain recrudescence of thefts. With Fascism there returned to the port the *"Confidente"* or *"intermediario"* or *"sub-contractor,"* a parasitic figure whom the port organisations had succeeded in putting to flight. There are more dock-workers than formerly. And the "Autonomous Port Consortium" has been for more than a year under the control of a Royal Commissioner.

8. *Public Debt.* The public debt has, naturally, also been a refractory subject for the magic wand. Although the exceptional war expenditure has definitely come to an end, the debt has continued to increase, as is shown by the following table, from which the debt on account of fiduciary circulation, already dealt with (section 3), has been excluded.

Debt	At September 30, 1922 Million lire	At September 30, 1923 Million lire
Consolidated ...	44,451	44,446
Redeemable ...	4,915	4,862
Long-term bonds ...	7,499	11,033
Ordinary bonds ...	24,570	24,163[1]
Other advances ...	410	548
Total internal debt ...	81,845	85,052
External debt, in gold lire	21,811	22,138

9. *Budget Deficits.* The apologists for Fascism have spread the fable that only the Fascist Government "had succeeded in bringing the State budget within sight of balancing, by bringing the deficit down with a rush from the many milliards of past years to the very few of the current year."

The truth is that the approach to balancing preceded Fascism, and was in large part the consequence of the cessation of the extraordinary expenditure due to the war. When this is taken into account it is at once clear, as the following table shows, that the Fascist Government has made and is making very little improvement over 1921-22.

[1] This reduction, by means of the issue of long-term bonds, was begun by the preceding Government, which had reduced the figure by nearly two milliards, from 26,837 milliards on April 19, 1922, to the figure shown above. During the early months of 1922, moreover, the Bonomi and Facta Governments reduced the interest on the annual bonds from 6 to 5 per cent., realising an economy of over 200 millions a year. No reduction has so far been announced by the Fascist Government, despite the boasted improvement in conditions and the reduced needs of the State.

	Total ascertained deficit Million lire	Exceptional war expenditure, now ended Million lire	Net normal deficit Million lire	Net anticipated deficit Million lire
1920-21	17,409	12,160	5,249	
1921-22	15,760	12,505	3,255	
1922-23	3,041	?	3,041 (?)	
1923-24	—	—	—	2,616[1]

10. *Taxation Revenue.* Relief was promised to those taxpayers who, before the arrival of Fascism, had organised taxation strikes; and on the other hand the Fascist press published under big headlines, in July, 1923, the news that there was to be an increase of 1,800 millions in the revenue.

The truth is that the taxation revenue, after the great post-war expansion due to the depreciation of the lira and to the necessity of meeting the new burdens left behind by the war, is now at the level reached by the provision made by past Governments, and is tending naturally to a settled figure. The official revenue figures are as follows:

	Million lire
1920-21	11,069
1921-22	12,795
1922-23	12,781
January to October, 1922	10,782
,, 1923	10,716

Further amounts have to be added of 1,059 millions in 1921-22 and 1,208 in 1922-23 for the difference between the values of the paper and the gold lira, paid in respect of customs duties payable in gold.

Thus in all 14 MILLIARDS of taxation was paid in each of the last two years, compared with 2 MILLIARDS before

[1] Already this figure has been increased, additional expenditure amounting to 400 millions having been decreed; the Ministerial Estimate of November, 1923, indicated an anticipated deficit of 2,913 millions.

the war. It is to THIS GREAT EFFORT, made almost entirely since the war (in 1919-20 we had nearly reached $7\frac{1}{2}$ milliards), and made in the face of the economic crisis already begun, THAT ITALY MAINLY OWES THE STABILITY OF HER CURRENCY AND THE APPROACH TO A BALANCED BUDGET.

The Socialists claim the honour of having stimulated the past Governments to adopt this course; while the Fascists excited against the financial provision made the bitterest opposition of the possessing classes; organised taxpayers' strikes, and secured the arming and subsidising of the first bands of the civil guerilla warfare.

And while Fascism thus took advantage of these classes' intolerance of taxation to carry it into power, to-day it is making capital out of the beneficent results of the taxation which it opposed and obstructed, by pretending that the credit for them is its own!

Under the Fascist Government the burden of taxation is continuing to fall, and to fall more heavily than ever, on consumption rather than on wealth, as is shown by the following table, based on official data for the first ten months of 1923 :—

Yield of taxation :

Direct	...	3,692 millions,	or 32%	ON WEALTH.
On exchange		1,093 ,,	or about 10%.	
On consumption		3,054 ,,	) or 58%	
Monopolies		2,737 ,,	} ON	
Customs		900 ,,	) CONSUMPTION.	

PART II.

ACTS OF THE FASCIST GOVERNMENT.

I.—The Abuse of Decree Laws.

The evil and danger of legislation by decree were summed up as follows by Signor Tittoni, as President of the Senate, in the sitting of April 3, 1922, when the Senate was opposing the abuse of this expedient at the hands of the Government of the day :

"Save for quite exceptional cases, the decree law is the fruit of lack of foresight and preparation, and of the impulsiveness and precipitateness which are among the greatest of dangers.   .   .   .

"The decree law is the tortuous method to which those classes have recourse, and those temporary or permanent associations of particular interests, which aspire to winning advantages at the expense of other classes of the community, advantages which they would fail to obtain by the straightforward method of legality.   .   .   .

"The decree law serves Governments as a means of extricating themselves from their embarrassments at difficult moments   .   .   .   but the budget of the State pays dearly for the momentary tranquillity so secured."

On May 31 the Senate passed the following resolution, which was accepted by the Government :

"The Senate, convinced of the necessity of placing restraints on the use of decree laws.   .   .   ."

The following figures show the number of
Decree Laws Promulgated.

Annual average, 1901 to 1911 (period of free institutions and of Socialist influence)   ...   4

Annual average, 1915 to 1921 (exceptional war
    and post-war period)   419

During the eight months of the Facta Ministry   103

During the year of Fascist rule (apart from about
    800 decrees issued under the Plenary Powers
    law)   517

That is, no Government has made such extensive and deplorable use of decree laws as the Fascist Government.

Irregular Decrees.

During the year the Corte dei Conti rejected, and
    subsequently registered only under reserve,
    more than   ...   .   decrees   500

That is, no Government has made such irregular and illegitimate use of decree laws as the Fascist Government.

II.—TAXATION POLICY.

The Fascist Programme. On the eve of the 1919 elections Mussolini declared that—

"One of the principal demands in the Fascist programme is the decimation of wealth, the confiscation of war-time excess profits, and a drastic levy on capital." (Milan, November 11, 1919.)

In the Fascist programme put forward in July, 1920, by the Central Fascist Committee (Mussolini, Bolzoni, Rossi, Arpinati, Farinacci, etc.), the following were included as immediate demands :

"(a) A heavy extraordinary levy on capital, progressive in character, to have the form of a real partial expropriation of all wealth, and to be payable within a very short period ;

"(b) The sequestration of all property of the religious Congregations, and the abolition of all the episcopal revenues, which constitute an enormous charge upon the nation and a privilege of a few persons ;

" (c) The revision of all contracts for war supplies, and the confiscation of excess war profits left unproductive;

"(d) Heavy inheritance duties."

The Fascist achievements are the direct opposite of the programme.

(a) The decree law No. 1431 of November 10, 1922, issued immediately after the accession of the Fascist Government—by way of an immediate return for its supporters—abrogated the law which required the inscription on all securities of the owners' names; such securities were thus enabled to escape from all control by the taxation authorities.

(b) On November 6, 1922, the National-Fascist Under-Secretary of the Treasury declared to the Paris "Journal" that "The confiscation of war profits must be abrogated"; but as this revenue was a necessity for the budget, only the largest and most obstinate firms were spared—those firms which were the only ones in Italy which had still paid nothing three years after the cessation of the levy.

(c) The Minister of Finance has described the levy on capital as "exceedingly stupid"; and he issued circulars directing that the valuations and transactions should be "as equitable, rapid and considerate as possible" (Riv. Fin. P.S., May, 1922)—that is, of course, for the capitalist taxpayer.

(d) The tax on directors and managers of Joint Stock Companies has been halved.

(e) The tax on perfumery and jewellery has been halved.

(f) Foreign capital invested in Italian industries has been declared exempt from taxation—by the very people who had protested so loudly against the harmful intrusion of French and German capital.

(g) The inheritance duty has been declared a piece

of demagogy; and the principle of "proprietà quiritaria" [1] has been re-established.

This same Fascist Ministry, which declared in the 1921 election that "The rights of property must be regarded as a simple question of administration in the interests of the collectivity; no more. The rights of property as conceived by the Romans are to-day a privilege which should no longer exist" (Verona, May 4, 1921)—once arrived at power, has abolished the succession duty within families, on the following ground: "Fascism is also, and above all, indissolubly bound up with respect for the family and for the Roman conception of property." (Decree No. 1802, August 20, 1923.)

Under this provision the State has renounced 200 million lire a year paid by the richest citizens, and the opportunity of attaining by more rigorous investigation at least 400 millions, which are wanted for balancing the budget.

(h) Up to the present [2] every provision making progressive the existing direct taxation has been postponed. These provisions were decreed on November 26, 1919, and the postponement of their application is a practical acknowledgement of sympathy with the resolutions passed by associations of the leading industrialists and capitalists.

To make good the reduction of the contributions of capital and of the richest classes, the Fascist Government, the moment it arrived at power, instituted for the

---

[1] A fundamental principle of Roman law, under which property transferred to direct descendants was exempt from taxation on passing.—*Trans.*

[2] The complementary taxation has just (end of December, 1923) been announced as intended to be put into operation as from January, 1925; the surcharge is raised in theory to 10 per cent., but in practice will be less than 5 per cent., and less than the surcharge already in force in 1919.

17

first time taxation of all *wages of employees* of the State, the provincial and communal authorities, and railway, tramway and shipping companies (Decrees Nos. 1660 and 1661, November 16 and December 21, 1922), deducting on an average 10 per cent.; it has instituted fresh taxation of the incomes of small farmers, and maintained the tax of 20 lire on vineyard produce despite the reduction in prices.

III.—Customs Policy.

The Fascist Minister of Finance loves to declare that he is of "Free Trade leanings," and his apologists have found proof of this in the suspension of the duty on sugar, in the correction of an erroneous duty on flour, and in the acceptance by decree of certain reductions on foodstuffs proposed in Parliamentary Committee.

The proof of the contrary is found in the following facts:

The Fascist Government has refused (a) to suppress the duty on grain; (b) to reduce the duty on rice; (c) to suppress the protective duty on flour; (d) to reduce the duties on grapes and wine; (e) has refused all proposed reductions on textiles, wool and cotton; (f) has not yet carried out the request made by resolution of the Chamber for an enquiry into wool duties; (g) has not given effect to the resolution of the Chamber in favour of suppressing the duty on pig iron, modifying the premiums on manufactures, and correspondingly reducing the duties on all metal and engineering products; (h) has not yet put into execution the resolution of the Chamber in favour of the suppression of the duty on copper and its derivatives; (i) has negatived similar proposals in regard to agricultural machinery, clocks, etc.; butter, cheese, soap; oil; cement, glass, and other building material; chemical and medicinal products, etc.

IV.—ECONOMIC POLICY.

(A) *State Intervention in Private Enterprise.*

Mussolini, as leader of the Fascists, defined the Fascist programme as follows in his first speech to the Chamber, on June 21, 1921 :

"The State must be restricted to its purely juridical and political functions. The State should give us a police, a system of justice, an army, a foreign policy. All the rest, even secondary education, must be restored to the field of activity of the individual . . . We have enough State Socialism already."

And one of Signor Mussolini's Under-Secretaries, expounding the Government programme on February 4, 1923, declared that—

"The Government will bring back our financial legislation within the bounds of its classic content, which excludes dangerous interventions in private enterprise and at the same time closes the State treasury to the unending swarm of parasites who in these latter years have been emptying it."

The actions of the Fascist Government have not corresponded to its professions, as the following examples show.

(a) *The Salving of the Ansaldo Firm.* The decree law of June 14, 1923, sanctioned the agreement between the Government and the Ansaldo Company, concluded in February, under which public funds were applied to the *refloating of this private enterprise,* whose speculations and sunk capital had been the principal cause of the crash of the Banca di Sconto, which was allowed to go into liquidation.

The chief result was the breaking up of the vertical concern built up by the Ansaldo Company, which had included the mines of Cogne, the works at Cornigliano, and the firm's shipyards. Rival groups were thus enabled to gain control of the various sections of the concern, to the advantage of rival companies and banks.

The State became a shareholder in the first group, Ansaldo-Cogne, bringing in 72 millions of *cash,* against 78 millions' worth of shares allocated to the creditors for works constructed, and further *taking up* 41½ *millions of mortgage bonds.* No. 135 of the "Agenzia Economica" contains a notice of the appointment of Commendatore Rosboch, a member of the Cabinet, to the board of the new Company; and of the fact that a combination with the Fiat Company was envisaged. There is also talk of a combination with the French firm of Giraud, that is, with Creusot.

The State has also undertaken to pay 22 millions to the builders of the six Battisti steamers, who are holding the vessels *for their own private account,* although they were not entitled to more than a small part of this subsidy.

The State has further recognised the right of the same private Company to a subsidy of 900 lire per ton in respect of certain other steamers, although they are not to be completed until 1924 instead of 1923, as provided by the Bellotti decree.[1]

The State has also undertaken to have 230 locomotives repaired in the works of the private Ansaldo Company, without prior settlement of prices, and without obtaining competitive offers from other firms.

The State is further committed to an annual contribution to the private Ansaldo Company, on consideration of the maintenance by the latter of certain plant in efficiency and of the plant being held at the disposal of the Government. The amount of the contribution will be fixed by a Commission; no effective equivalent for it is being rendered.

The State has accepted by arrangement the sum of 52 millions in lieu of all taxes and duties, ordinary and upon excess profits, due from the Ansaldo Company in

[1] See section (f), page 23.

respect of many milliards' worth of production and profits during and since the war.

(b) *Acquisition of Industrial Concerns.* On April 29, 1923, the Fascist Government decided to purchase 18,000 shares in the Mineral Oil Refinery of Fiume, for 8,300,443 lire. Signor Monti, an engineer belonging to the Fascist technical committees, had stated that "The acquisition of the shares, considered as a commercial transaction, can only create a spurious prosperity, injurious to the finances of the State, and dangerous to the establishment itself."

As a director representing the Government on the board of the Refinery there has been nominated Commendatore Rosboch, a former bank employee, who is not resident in Fiume, and has never been associated with the oil industry, but who had negotiated the purchase; among other "oil experts" appointed to the board were Massimo Rocca, Dino Grandi, Iginio Magrini.[1]

(c) *Intervention in Banking Affairs.* At the end of 1921 the Banca di Sconto was allowed to crash, but in 1923 the Fascist Government, intervening in the very field of private enterprise in which it had professed that it ought not to intervene, came to the rescue of the Banco di Roma.

The fact is disclosed by the reports of the Bank itself; but *it is not revealed by any law or decree.* This shows that a few persons are able to dispose of milliards of public money, even in the interest of private concerns, without either public or parliamentary control.[2]

The facts are, however, revealed indirectly by decrees

[1] Well-known Fascist political leaders.—*Trans.*

[2] In recognition of this favour the representatives of the board of the Banco di Roma gave a public assurance to the meeting of shareholders on September 29, 1923, that "the work of the board will be inspired by a sense of the deepest responsibility and *of gratitude to the Fascist Government.*" They forgot to add that payment was being made not by the Fascist Government but by the Italian nation.

21

on other matters which have been issued in the past year.

(i) The decrees of January 2 and September 27, 1923, renewed the privilege of the three banks of issue until 1930.

No question is more delicate than this, and none merited more attentive prior examination in the Finance Committees of the Senate and Chamber. Instead, recourse has been had without further ado to decree laws, not covered by the plenary powers of the Government; and there have been particular circumstances not always laudable. Owing to irregularities in the publication of the decrees there was very heavy speculation, in the course of which immense sums were won and lost. An enquiry into the scandal was opened —by the Government itself; and naturally nothing came of it.

(ii) These decrees also laid down that the tax due from the banks for the paper money issued beyond a certain limit, instead of being paid over to the State, should be retained, as to three parts of it, until 1930, as a reserve to make good possible losses of the banks. It will be possible for over two milliards to accumulate in this period in the hands of the Banca d'Italia, which, at the bidding of the Fascist Government, may use this public money to rescue private concerns and to cover possible losses.

There has been nothing so far to show that the directors of the embarrassed banks have been required to make good the banks' losses. Senator Marconi, a member of the board of the Banca di Sconto, was admitted to membership of the Fascist party in October, 1923. In November he was absolved from all liability.

(d) *Unlimited Access of the Heavy Industries to the Resources of the Banks of Issue.* Under the decree law No. 587 of March 29, 1923, the limit up to which the *Consorzio privato per sovvenzioni su valori indus-*

triali is allowed to draw upon the banks of issue for credit, apart from the subventions to which it is already entitled, was raised above the original figure of one milliard lire.

Thus a quasi-monopoly of credit, half State, half private, withdrawn from all public control, has been set up by the authority of the State, working with public money, and in a position to influence the fiduciary circulation, which is the first element in the cost of living for every citizen.

The *Consorzio* has the right of rediscounting with the Bank of Italy at $1\frac{1}{2}$ per cent. below the official rate of discount.

For the rest, the rate of discount in Italy has often been fixed at an unduly low figure to the advantage of limited groups.

(e) *Funds for ex-Austrian Industrialists.* Under Royal decree No. 2148 of September 27, 1923, the Fascist Government granted a loan of 138 million lire for 35 years at 4 per cent. to certain great industrialists of Trieste. The loan constitutes a settlement for alleged war damage, compensation for which was refused to firms which were predominantly foreign in ownership and administration.

An analogous project was submitted on May 31, 1922, by the Facta Government, but met with such objections in the Finance Committee that it was not then passed.

(f) *A Further 55 Millions for Shipbuilders.* On September 25, 1921, Signor Bellotti, Minister of Industry and Commerce, granted a subsidy of 125 million lire to shipbuilders. The Finance Committee declared that the shipbuilders were in no way entitled to this, and that only a certain sum, *within* a total of 125 millions, could be allowed in the case of shipbuilders who had completed vessels before June 30, 1921, and had obtained a promise of subsidies. Yet the decree was promulgated, and with a change in the provision fixing a maximum amount.

The new Fascist regime, however, has not only not put a stop to the bad practice; it has extended it, first admitting to the benefits of the subsidy steam vessels completed in 1924 (Royal decree No. 879, March 22, 1923), then increasing the subsidy fund by a further 55 millions (Royal decree No. 1344, June 14). Thus the 24 vessels mentioned in the Bill presented in the Chamber on December 13, 1921, have been nearly doubled.

Let not the taxpayer imagine that in this way the State has become owner of a larger number of vessels. No! The vessels are all in private ownership; they were also already in large part completed; the State has only the satisfaction of having reimbursed to private individuals virtually the whole of the present value of the vessels!

(g) *Building Subsidies.* The Fascist press carried on one of its most vehement campaigns against the State subsidies for the construction of dwellings for workpeople and employees.

But though on the arrival of the Fascist Government in power this policy was brought generally to an end, a few interesting and singular exceptions were made. There were granted—

(1) Under decree No. 105 of January 11, 1923, for co-operative housing for journalists, a subsidy of 270,000 lire per annum;

(2) Under decree No. 1044 of April 22, 1923, for dwellings for employees of the Foreign Ministry, 200,000 lire per annum.

Two further decrees, No. 1932 of July 12, and No. 2118 of September 10, 1923, authorised the railway administration to grant loans of 40 million lire for housing construction for the railway co-operatives.

The president of one of these co-operatives happens to be Mussolini's secretary.

(h) *State Subsidy for Shipping Lines.* Under decree law No. 1998 of September 10, 1923, the Fascist Government revived this lamentable practice, with a temporary subsidy of 1,610,000 lire for the line from Palermo to Tunis.

(i) *Loans to Private Companies.* Under decree law No. 1386 of June 17, 1923, the Fascist Government granted Treasury bonds up to 100 million lire to the Società Italiana per le F.S. del Mediterraneo (Italian Co. for the Mediterranean State Railways).

(B) *Opportunities Given to Private Speculators.*

Suppression of the Enquiry into War-time Expenditure. The Fascist programme of 1920 contained a demand for "the revision of all contracts for war supplies." But Fascism was hardly in power before it issued a decree (No. 1487 of November 19, 1922) suppressing the Committee of Enquiry into war expenditure, which had proceeded to the revision of contracts and had restored to the State some hundreds of millions illegitimately extorted from it.

Sicilian Railway Concessions. Under two agreements of March 21, 1923 (not published until October 11 !) a concession for the construction of 800 kilometres of Sicilian railways was granted, one-half to a certain Signor Nicolini and a Signor Romano, on behalf of a Company to be formed, and the other half to a General Public Works and Services Company, of which Signor Biraghi, a member of the Superior Council of Public Works, is consulting engineer.

The cost of the work is about a milliard lire; the concession has none of the usual characteristics : it is not for a definite object (there are no plans ; it has not been decided whether the lines are to be of normal or narrow gauge ; the 400 kilometre sections may be reduced or increased ; the route is not determined) ;

there is no guarantee to the State; there is no time limit for completion of the work. Only this is clearly determined : the right is to be enjoyed, for no consideration in return, by simple private individuals lacking any sort of title (unless, perhaps, the friendship of the Minister), of the monopoly of a work of construction of a value running into a milliard, and capable of extension *ad lib.* (a right on which the concessionaires may trade, drawing sensational profits); and of a commission of 8 per cent. in addition to the payment of the costs of flotation and of all possible and imaginable general expenses : a small *douceur* of 80 millions !

Sugar. In 1922, in consideration of an exceedingly high protective duty, the sugar refiners undertook to supply the whole of the 1922-23 crop at 575 lire the quintal. The Government maintained the duty and the fixed price until the end of May, 1923, thus preventing the entry into the country of foreign sugar, which was cheap in the autumn of 1922.

In May, 1923, protection had become superfluous, as foreign sugar was dearer than Italian. The Government then abolished the duty, but at the same time it arbitrarily and secretly allowed the refiners and dealers to sell their sugar at prices higher than the agreed price, on the ground that the Italian crop was insufficient for the year's consumption. Refiners and dealers were thus enabled to dispose of some 700,000 quintals of native sugar at prices averaging 65 lire the quintal above the fixed price.

The Government told the Chamber that it had helped to regulate prices by admitting German sugar on reparation account; but, as the Socialists foresaw, this sugar only began to arrive too late to be of effect.

Thus, first the Government inflicted on the whole nation a loss of several millions of gold lire by preventing the admission of cheap foreign sugar into the country;

Then, in contravention of a precise undertaking, it put nearly fifty million lire, taken from the consumers, into the pockets of the sugar speculators;

And finally, it now finds itself burdened with over 40,000 quintals of German sugar, paid for at a price which is making its resale difficult.

Cost of Living. Fascism has destroyed the co-operatives and the communal authorities and voluntary associations which aimed at keeping down the cost of living. But in June, 1923, the Minister of Commerce set up a Committee which reported that "the State must encourage, intensify and co-ordinate the action of the administration and the local authorities in connection with the organisation and discipline of the markets, on the one hand, and the efforts, on the other hand, of provincial and communal authorities, co-operatives, chambers of commerce and private individuals to secure the most economical means of supply"; and the Minister proposed "to set up authorities to control the supplies of the more important centres." (June 22, 1923.) Thus, in substance it was proposed to return to the system which had been destroyed.

Actually, however, nothing was done. The markets were not supervised. Order was not introduced into the system of supplies. Authorities were not constituted; and speculation triumphed.

Here, indeed, is a specimen of local Fascist methods, from Carrara: The Fascist High Commissioner assembles all the marble quarrying firms, deplores the unrestrained competition, establishes a price, "prohibiting any sort of reduction, direct or indirect," and threatens any who sell at cheaper rates with "branding as guilty of improper trading, with all the logical and practical consequences . . . assuring his hearers that he has the support of the Government. . . . Agreements already concluded at lower rates are to be

27

denounced and annulled." ("Alalà," Fascist daily paper for the province of Carrara, February 24, 1923.)

Increase of Rents. Under decree No. 8 of January 7, 1923, the restrictions on increases in the rents of dwellings were declared no longer operative. In face of the agitation aroused, the Government added provisions for setting up local arbitral commissions, to determine rents without appeal, dwelling by dwelling. These commissions are dominated by the local Fascist groups.

The decrees of September 10, 1923, No. 2023, and December 3, 1922, No. 1583, permitted increases in the rent of agricultural holdings.

Liquidation of Reconstruction Authority. Decree No. 2022, of September 24, 1923, ordered the liquidation of the Ente Unione Edilizia, the authority which had dealt with reconstruction work, especially in the areas devastated by earthquake. It is evident how much harm is done by the rapid closing down of so important an authority. Certain financial journals, on the other hand, have expressed readiness to see a private speculative company set up in its place; a company in which a leading part would be played by certain friends of members of the Government.

Cession of Waterway. Under decree No. 696, of March 8, 1923, the State canals of the Novarese and Lomellina were leased to a local Joint Stock Company.

Life Assurance. Decrees Nos. 1638, November 16, 1922, and 966, April 29, 1923, prolonged the right of private Life Assurance Companies (including those in which the capital was not wholly in Italian hands) to carry on business; although such business was to have passed into the hands of the State last year.

State Supplies. (a) The Ministerial Decree of January 13, 1923, which has not yet been published, and has already been once rejected by the Corte dei Conti as irregular, granted 28,835,996 lire to the

Orlando firm at Leghorn, as indemnification *and additional payment beyond the contract scale,* for the construction of torpedo-boat destroyers, and remitted the penalties for delay in delivery. The concessions were obtained on the score of strikes, lock-outs, and demonstrations—under the old regime.

(b) The Royal decree, No. 62, January 24, 1923, which instituted the office of Commissioner for aeronautics, exempted the Commissioner from the legislative provisions in force in regard to administration and accounts (Art. 3). The official announcement added that the supply of material would be entrusted exclusively to certain firms known to the Fascist Commissioner for their "proved patriotism." We do not know whether these are the same firms which at that date were assembled at Genoa to constitute the Associazione Industriale di Aeronautica, were received by Mussolini, and obtained from him, as was announced in the papers, "assurances" (January 15-18, 1923). Or whether the reference is to firms who are lavishly supporting certain of the great Fascist journals.

(c) The High Commissioner for the railways has boasted of an economy effected in the uniforms of the railway servants. In point of fact the supply was entrusted to a firm by private arrangement, without taking other offers into consideration. This firm was supplied with the whole stock of clothing material in the possession of the State railways; and in respect of its distribution to the railwaymen the firm was granted a commission of 22 per cent. on its value, which, naturally, will be paid—by the railwaymen!

(d) A Rome paper has stated that the High Commissioner for railways rescinded a contract for the disposal of war stocks, under decree of September 20, 1923; but that on the 27th of the same month he concluded a fresh contract with the same firm, with a reduction of price from 1,672,000 to 1,200,000 lire, without endeavouring to obtain competitive offers; the Commissioner actually allowed, on his own authority, a further discount of 8 per cent. It appears also that the co-operative with which the deal was made was a fictitious one, and that the material actually went to a well-known industrialist.

General Pizzone, inspector of army corps at Milan, who exposed the scandal, was attacked on the evening after the exposure by a secretary of the railway Commissariat.

Revocation of the Peasants' Right to the Lands Occupied. The decree of January 11, 1923, abolished the grants which had been made to the peasants of those lands, belonging to the latifundia of the great landowners, of which, over large parts of Italy, they had taken forcible possession.

In Sicily alone, the Bank of Sicily had financed nearly 100,000 acres of occupied land, granting credit to the amount of 700,000 lire for the payment of octroi duties, five million lire for collective purchases, and, for these and other purposes, a total sum of 34 millions, virtually without incurring any loss at all.

V.—LABOUR POLICY.

Workers' Organisations. In many parts of Italy, especially in rural districts, working class organisations which are not under Fascist control *have no possibility of existence.* In the large towns and in certain districts in which the Fascist monopoly is less absolute, the organisations still exist, but enjoy only a very restricted freedom of action. (See the chronicle of facts, in Part IV.) *Nowhere* can meetings of any importance be held, still less public ones. In general agreements and pacts concerning labour conditions are impossible; conditions are laid down by the Fascist Corporations and imposed on the workers, even where nine-tenths of the workers organised by the Corporations still remain members of other organisations.

In reply to the remonstrances of the organisers of the General Confederation of Labour (who in most cases are members of the Socialist Party—the P.S.U.), the head of the Government has repeatedly let it be understood that "the liberty of organisations will depend on the attitude of their leaders" (official communication, November 19, 1923), that is that the latter would have in substance to abjure their political faith and ignore the deliberations of the Party.

In vain has the Confederation, since the split in October, 1922, between the "maximalist" and the "unitary" Socialists, declared itself independent of all parties; in vain did its general secretary repeat that declaration in the Chamber, in reply to the remarks addressed personally to him by the Under-Secretary for the Interior. The Confederation has been forced to declare publicly, in its resolutions of August and November, 1923, that the civic liberties are lacking which are a prior condition for any free trade union activity.

Capitalist Organisations. The semi-official "Volta" news agency issued this communication on November 17, 1922:

"It is recognised [by the Fascist Government] that the greater part of the industrial forces of Italy is grouped in the Federation of Industries, and it is declared that there is no desire to cause splits or any diminution in the technical or moral efficiency of the Federation."

The communication added that "the relations between the President and Secretary of the employers' industrial Federation and the head of the Government, Signor Mussolini, are more than cordial."

Fascist Corporations. Whether they like it or not, the workers are *compelled* to join the Fascist Corporations. In the rural districts any worker who does not belong is refused employment and *boycotted*. The internal organisation of the Corporations is constituted on anti-democratic bases; there are no elections of the managing body; the officials are all appointed from above. The Corporation emanates from and is dependent on the political *fasci* (Fascist political groups).

Theoretically, "in Fascist syndicalism, the workers, technicians and work-givers constitute a harmonious whole with a common discipline" (Mussolini, in the Grand Fascist Council, March 14, 1923). Actually, business men and shopkeepers, representatives of the farmers, and so on, have entered the Fascist Corporations. As mentioned above, the industrialists have obtained complete autonomy; the autonomy of the Agrarian Federation, on the other hand, has been contested.

The Préfects are completely subservient to the employers' and workers' organisations favoured by the Government. The Prefect of Genoa, for instance, has issued a decree requiring shipowners "at all times to allow free access on board to the representatives of the seamen's organisation of which Giulietti is secretary."

This last fact is connected with a curious case of exceptional treatment. The only non-Fascist workers' organisation which has been respected up to now is that of the "Garibaldi Seamen's Co-operative," of which the secretary, Giulietti, is a protégé of d'Annunzio. The Fascist Press launched a bitter campaign against it, and from the first the Commissioner of Mercantile Marine declared, in Mussolini's name, "that no agreement had ever been entered into between the Fascists and Giulietti; and that a committee had been appointed in order that all relations might be broken off as soon as possible with the Garibaldi Co-operative."

However, owing to d'Annunzio's protection, this Seamen's Federation has not been touched, and the Fascists themselves have been ordered to re-enter it;

the Government has taken part for more than a year in the endeavour to bring to an end the dispute between seamen and owners, and has upheld the contracts, so obnoxious to the Fascists, with the Garibaldi Co-operative; in the end, in face of the resistance of the owners, the Government has declared that

"Considering that the explanation given reveals a spirit of equity and readiness to collaborate in the pact proposed by the Seamen's Federation, the Commissioner of Marine, in the name of the Government, has determined to put into execution the clauses of the pact which concern it." (Official communication of November 4, 1923.)

But still further changes and surprises are expected.[1]

Right to Strike. The free [2] organisations have in practice *no* right of striking. In July, 1923, the free organisation of the Roman bricklayers proclaimed a strike, but the police and Fascist militia intervened; 250 workers were arrested, and over 130 made to leave Rome.

On the other hand, members of the Fascist Corporations can always strike; or rather, the strike is not called on their initiative but ordered by the Fascist leaders (*e.g.,* in the Monfalcone hipyard, March 22; Spoleto cotton mill, April 2, etc.) Not only this, but the leaders have initiated those very invasions of estates and occupations of factories, steamships, etc., for which so much execration was hurled at—the Bolshevists! (*e.g.,* April 30, 1923, occupation of S.S. Tiepolo at Genoa; May 31, occupation of estates in the Novarese (Province of Novara); June 29, occupation of the Officine Meridionale ["Southern Factories"] at Naples, etc.) Or threats and violence

[1] Early this year, under the pressure of the shipowners, the Fascist Government appointed Royal Commissioners to control the Seamen's Federation and the Garibaldi Seamen's Co-operative.—*Trans.*

[2] That is, free from Fascist control.—*Trans.*

have even been employed against employers. For instance, the Fascist Federation of the Bolognese resolved "to proceed Fascistically against the non-fulfilment of their engagements by the employers" (June 30, 1923) ; and in execution of the resolution Count Malvasia-Torelli di Sasso was beaten. But behind these sanctions for non-fulfilment of engagements, there was something more than usual; to wit, a refusal to adhere or give contributions to Fascism !

The Fascist paper, "Ora," of Pesaro, published this communication on September 22 : "Certain owners have offered us sums which, in proportion to the capital which Fascism has safeguarded for them, are no more than one-millionth per cent. In view, therefore, of the fact that the past system of collection of funds has yielded us nothing, I warn all owners in the Province of Pesaro and Urbino that I shall tax them in proportion to their capital, in such a way as definitely to systematise the financial situation of Fascism in our province."

Co-operatives. The non-Fascist Co-operatives have been destroyed or compelled to accept Fascist intervention. This is admitted in so many words : "We will repeat once more : The Co-operatives which have been burnt down have been well burnt down, for only in this way was it possible definitely to make sure that elements in the co-operative movement were not serving as blind tools of an anti-national political party." (Postiglione, head of the Fascist Co-operatives, September 12, 1923.)

And, for example, Mussolini's paper, the "Popolo d'Italia," reports :

"Bollate, December 15. An agreement has been arrived at, in the following terms : The managing body of the Co-operative to be dismissed, and a meeting to be called for the appointment of fresh managers, to be approved by the Fascio" (the local Fascist political organisation).

The Prefects and the authorities have intervened

everywhere to close down the non-Fascist Co-operatives. Even the great Co-operative Union of Milan and Co-operative Alliance of Turin, etc., have had to submit to Government intervention. The conditions imposed for allowing the Co-operatives of Reggio to continue to exist included this : "The managers shall be replaced by men approved by the Prime Minister." (Stefani news agency, August 15, 1923.)

At Turin the Prefect appointed, by decree, as administrators of the Workers' General Association, individuals not belonging to the Association ; and he required the *palazzo sociale* (club buildings) of the Association to be sold within a year.

To legalise all the arbitrary Government interference in workers' organisations and co-operatives, especially those of Molinella (see Part V.), the Government announced at the beginning of October, 1923, a decree to give the political authorities control of *Società di fatto* (societies engaged in practical work). But the announcement of this enormity has as yet had no further sequel.

On the other hand, the Fascist Co-operatives are demanding from the State privileges which the others did not have, namely : "reservation of part of the Government contracts at the approved or higher rates ; assistance to cover the deficit on the Consumers' Co-operative Societies ; authority to use deposits as security," etc. (Meeting of Fascist Co-operatives, September 30, 1923.)

The destruction of free Co-operation has fulfilled one of the dearest dreams of private shopkeepers and speculators, and has removed one of the most efficacious checks on rising prices.

Abolition of Labour Day. In decree No. 933 of April 19, 1923, the Fascist Government declared that "the holiday on May 1 is suppressed, and all the agreements entered into between employers and workers for a day's

35

holiday on that date are to be put into application on April 21 (the Fascist holiday) and not on May 1." The police and the Fascist Militia are required to prosecute all workers who may celebrate May day, and to compel the employers to dismiss them.

Working Hours. For some time a draft bill for the eight-hour working day was before Parliament; it was the result of long and careful elaboration by the Superior Council of Labour, and was accepted by all the representatives of employers and workers.

Following the protest of Signor Turati, the Socialist Deputy, the Fascist Government undertook to deal with the question. Instead, however, it issued the Royal decree No. 692, of March 15, 1923, and the governing regulations of September 10, 1923, which constitute a negation of the eight-hour day.

Such guarantees as the admission of the workers concerned to the controlling bodies, the equal representation of employers and workers, and so on, have been suppressed;

Work on board ship, in religious institutions, and for fixed wages in agriculture is excluded from the scope of the decree;

A *normal* addition of *two hours'* work is sanctioned;

The additional rate for overtime has been allowed to be reduced to 10 per cent., in place of the 25 per cent. or more already established in every Italian labour agreement and sanctioned by the Washington Convention;

Various devices, averagings and exceptions have been allowed which in fact annul the eight-hour day in agriculture and in a number of industries;

The intervention of the Labour Inspectorate is excluded, the penalties for infringements are reduced to trifling amounts; and so on.

In fact, the Government decree has not improved the conditions of labour of a single Italian worker.

In a number of cases, employers have taken advantage of the decree to propose worse terms than those already provided in existing agreements, either by reducing overtime rates or by calculating at ordinary rates periods and classes of work formerly paid at higher rates.

Social Insurance. (a) *Unemployment and Labour Exchanges.* The central and local offices have been suppressed. Nearly all the funds have been placed under the administration of a government commissioner. The workers have to pay their contributions, but have no say in the administration of their money. All the labour exchanges set up under decrees already in force have been suppressed; the mixed offices have been reduced. (Decree of February 4, 1923.)

(b) *Agricultural Accidents Insurance.* Workers over 65 and under 12 years of age have been excluded from compensation, while no legislative provision has been made to prohibit working outside these limits. The burden of insurance has been thrown, in whole or in part, on the small tenant working on his own account, the *métayer*, and the cultivator working for a share in the yield. The minimum degree of permanent invalidity entitling to compensation has been raised from 10 to 15 per cent. Small owners, *métayers*, tenants and their families have been excluded from grants for temporary incapacity, thus relieving the big landowners of the payment of insurance premiums. (Decree law of February 11, 1923.)

(c) *Sickness.* On November 16, 1922, the Council of Ministers made promises in regard to sickness insurance, but no further proposals have been brought forward to give effect to the promise.

(d) *Invalidity, Old Age and Unemployment Insurance.* In many districts the landowners have suspended their contributions. The Court of Cassation has declared invalid the decrees imposing contributions, on the ground that they have not been converted into laws; and accordingly the employers' contributions have everywhere been suspended. The Government has stood by idly in face of the virtual abolition of insurance.

Inspectorate of Labour Conditions. This is no longer functioning. The number of officials has been reduced to 26 for the whole of Italy. Accordingly, all the legislation for the protection of labour, of women and children, etc., is deprived of the one safeguard which remained after the destruction of the workers' organisations.

Sickness Insurance Committees in the new Provinces.
Unemployment Insurance Committees.
Unemployment and Labour Exchange Boards.
Arbitral Committees for Rural Labour.

These have also been closed down, or replaced by Government Commissioners.

Superior Council of Labour and Permanent Committee of Labour. These were the nuclei of the new labour legislation, and were capable of development into fresh and more highly developed forms. Instead, they have been suppressed without further ado under Royal decree No. 2125 of September 6, 1923; and in their place there has been set up a Superior Council of National Economy, on lines laid down in Royal decree No 2579 of December 2, 1923, which make it a purely bureaucratic organ, controlled exclusively by nominees of the Minister and directly dependent upon him. The administrative work of the Council will be under the direction of a permanent official. So the first germ of labour legislation and of the regularisation of the direct settlement of matters of mutual concern between employers and workers has been destroyed.

Ministry of Labour. Suppressed under Royal decree No. 915 of April 27, 1923, after the political crisis which arose out of the relations between the Catholic Popular Party and the Fascist Government.

National and International Representative Bodies.
In the State consultative bodies and the social insurance institutions (Superior Councils of Emigration, Public Assistance, Co-operation, National Accident Insurance Committee, Social Insurance Committee, etc.), the Government has replaced the representatives of the free workers' organisations by delegates from the Fascist Corporations, or has placed the former in a minority.

In the Conferences of the International Labour Office at Geneva, the Government has withdrawn the workers' representative formerly nominated by the General Confederation of Labour, and replaced him by a representative of the Fascist Corporations, which are mixed bodies containing representatives of workers and employers.

Arbitrary Dismissals. Under a series of decrees the State has set the example of discharging workers without any guarantee as to selection or procedure, or of investigation and opportunity for defence. (Decrees Nos. 87, January 25, 1923; 143 and 153, January 28; 945, April 14, for State employees; 2046, September 24, for employees of tramway and railway companies; 1177, May 27, for employees of local authorities.)

All these decrees exclude the workers from self-defence against illegality through recourse to the Council of State, which has been the normal recourse at all times against administrative injustice. In the case of railway companies, the decree allows appeal to the Minister of Public Works, whose decision is final; but only ten days is allowed for the presentation of the case to the Ministry, a time limit which in most cases renders the appeal impossible.

In the Government paper-money printing works at Turin, the regulations have been modified by imposing immediate discharge, without any sort of recompense for long years of service, as a punishment for the entirely new offences of "notorious 'subversivism', anti-constitutionalism, or anti-patriotism"! The same regulation has been introduced into the Government tobacco factories, with the addition of "immorality" in women.

VI.—PUBLIC SERVICES.

One of the loudest cries of the Fascists was that they would know how to apply the axe to the Government staffs and to simplify the public services.

Number of Employees. Instead of this, after a year we learn, from the report accompanying decree No. 2395, November 11, 1923, on the regulation of the public services, that the staff actually employed (excluding State railways and the army) numbered 115,591 and would be reduced after the impending changes to 110,447; while before the war the total number was 103,643. Thus the total reduction is less than 5 per cent.

It is true that Article 211 of the decree provides that by the end of 1925 there shall be a further reduction of 5 per cent., and a third 5 per cent. by the end of 1928. But all this is merely a paper promise; while the fact is that, in spite of the endless shouting about simplification, leasing, and winding-up of public services, there has only been effected a small reduction, roughly equal to that which the past Ministries had obtained with much less self-advertisement.

In the two Ministries over which Mussolini presides, the staffs have been increased, not diminished. That of the Ministry of the Interior has been increased from 6,891 to 8,145, apart from 1,503 subordinate officials. The staff of the Ministry of Foreign Affairs has increased from 384 in April, 1923, to 489.

Expenditure. As to expenditure, this same Ministerial Report makes the confession that it will be greater than formerly, allowing for all the cost-of-living bonuses, etc.; in other words, precisely the opposite of what the Fascists promised !

The extent of the increase is not mentioned. The report says it will not be "of great importance"; it appears, however, that it will be double the 100 millions which the Socialists demanded at one time—a demand for making which they were denounced as wreckers.

Salaries. The salaries of all grades formerly in receipt of at least 30 lire a day have been increased. The largest increases of all have gone to the higher grades, some salaries being doubled.

On the other hand, the lower categories remain without a change (Article 190) for the moment; but from time to time they will suffer *reductions* of salary, first through the absorption of the cost-of-living bonus of 780 lire per annum (Article 188), and later reductions of their actual salaries, as is shown in tables attached to the report. In a number of cases, especially among those who have served for many years, there will be an immediate loss, in order that the pensionable part of their salaries may be increased.

Espionage and political persecution have naturally been introduced into the Government service. The Minister of Finance has actually issued the following official circular :

"It is communicated for general information that in future the granting of annual leave of absence and other privileges of the subordinate staff will be in the hands of the Captain of the Royal Carabineers attached to this office. He will also be responsible for the mainten-ance of discipline, the supervision of the movements of the said staff, and the verification of the causes of absence on account of sickness or for other reasons" !

Political Oath. There has now been imposed upon the employees an oath not to belong to any of those parties which Fascism finds it convenient to qualify as "anti-national."

VII.—State Railways.

The Fascist Government has stated that the deficit of the State railways, estimated at 654 million lire for 1923-24, will be reduced to 374 millions, and to nothing in 1925.

Up to the present, however, we have had nothing but promises and speeches; there have been no precise details. The only document issued has been a little work distributed by the Railway Commissioner in August, 1923.

This booklet begins with defamations, unquestionably anti-national, of the Italian public of past years, members of which are said to have been "in the habit of travelling without a regular ticket," and to have paid "only in limited numbers for a ticket of admission to the stations," while "evil-doers committed every sort of criminal offence."

It is a fact that Fascist bands provided plentiful examples of travelling without payment, until at last the Government was compelled to issue a circular on the subject. It is a fact that in various parts of Italy, on occasions of Fascist celebrations, none of the participants who travelled by train paid their fares.

The Fascist Minister of Public Works was asked in Parliament how many free tickets had been issued during 1923, outside certain categories legally entitled to them, and how many free trains had been run. *As yet he has been unable to reply.*

Personnel. Under the old regime the railway staffs were reduced from 242,000 to 226,000. The reduction in 1921-22 alone amounted to 10,797 employees. (Report of Signor Alzona, Director-General of Railways, November 30, 1922.)

Under the new regime, according to the Commissioner's statement, the number has been reduced to 190,000, and it can be further reduced to 180,000.

Everyone was in agreement as to the necessity of

reducing the staff, which had been greatly increased since the war by large entries of ex-service men and of temporary workers (about 25,000) to make good the damage and deterioration on the lines during the war; and under the old regime the Chamber had unanimously passed a resolution in favour of better observance of the eight-hour day. But the present discharges are open to objection in the following respects :

(i) They have been resorted to as political or personal reprisals. Almost the whole of the first batch of discharges was made up of those who had taken part in Socialist associations or movements.

The Fascist daily, *Il Nuovo Paese,* wrote on February 3, 1923 : "A first batch of subversive railwaymen got rid of. . . . To-day begins what we will call the political purge. . . . This is a first group of railway servants, including the most uncompromising extremists."

(ii) The best elements were dismissed without cause shown. One man, discharged for 'insufficient output,' has the following certificate of character : "Maximum output, very great zeal, very high capacity. Has been doing two men's work for the past two years. 350 hours of unpaid overtime. Only ten days' sickness in many years' service." Another, re-employed by arrangement after a serious injury while on duty, has been discharged for 'insufficient output.' Another was discharged while doing superior duties to his own; he had 14 wounds in 28 months' service at the front, and bore the medal for valour. Another, who had served 11 years in a malarial region, was discharged for 'insufficient output' in the very week in which he received a gratuity granted by the Railway Commissioner for good work during 1923.

(iii) The discharged men have had no remedy, existing guarantees against injustice or even illegality being ignored.

(iv)   Instead of taking advantage of normal wastage, large numbers of young men have been discharged, representing a heavy pension charge on the State for many years to come.

Anyone, on the other hand, who wants to keep his post or to win rapid promotion or increase of salary, has only to declare himself a Fascist.   A typical case is that of Chiarini, a secretary in 1920, and at that time a candidate for membership of the "subversive" railwaymen's union.   Becoming instead adviser to the Fascist Commissioner, he is now well on the road to appointment as Director-General !

Fascist Militia.   While the non-Fascist personnel is being discharged or persecuted, there has been instituted on the railways a Fascist railway police, unique in the whole of the modern civilised world.

On its first institution it worked so well that it had to be broken up.   (Official communication of May 9, 1923.)

Now a second force has been instituted, seconded from the National Militia; its function was stated in the press on the same date, May 9, as follows : "There will be constituted special detachments of railway militia, for the purpose . . . of establishing among the great mass of railwaymen nuclei of proved veterans to irradiate Fascist propaganda" !

The chronicle of facts in Part IV. gives instances of injurious treatment of non-Fascist railwaymen (searches, invasion of clubs, punishments for political reasons), and even of railway passengers obnoxious to the Fascists.

The numbers of this militia and their conditions of service are not yet clear.   They are said to number 10,000 to 15,000, distributed in twelve legions; and from decree No. 2158 of September 27, 1923, it would appear that they receive railwaymen's pay, *plus* a special allowance. The Minister has been asked in Parliament, but *has not yet replied.*

Services Rendered by Staff. The High Commissioner makes much of alleged reductions in absences and improved services. All this can only be judged from the precise details when they are published.

Meanwhile the recurrence of delays in the train services (to such a degree that an official explanation had to be issued, November 9, 1923), and various collisions, etc., are not calculated to reassure.

Economies. Some have been effected simply to the injury of the staffs; such as the abolition of compensation for malaria, the suppression of soap and towels for the staffs, and so on.

Others are doubtful :—

(a) *Repairs to Rolling Stock.* An important part of this is automatic, since the first years after the war had immense arrears to make up.

A further automatic saving as against past years accrues from the falling prices, enabling contracts to be revised.

A third economy in expenditure is possible through allowing material to deteriorate. The Commissioner's promised economies are worth *nothing* unless he proves at the same time that the condition of railways and equipment is improving.

(b) *Coal :* 30 million lire is claimed to have been saved in six months. After the war, however, coal leaped up to 800 lire the ton; now it is about 220. In 1920-21 it averaged over 400. On a year's consumption of $2\frac{1}{2}$ million tons, even 100 lire less per ton means a saving of 250 *million lire.* A further recent advantage, owing to the invasion of the Ruhr, is the substitution of British for the greatly inferior German coal.

(c) *Metals.* The Commissioner admits that this is due to falling prices and reduced purchases.

(d) *Oils and Lubricants.* Again, falling prices. A further reduction is due to "consumption of stocks provided in the preceding year" (Torre Report).

(e) Finally, certain railway services have been leased to private industry, and to this extent the economy in personnel is only apparent.

Increased Revenue. (a) *Tariffs have been raised :* *Third class,* 15 per cent. ; *second class,* 6 per cent. ; *first class,* no increase.

(b) 134 *millions* is a mere transfer from postal to railway revenue.

(c) *Goods traffic* shows an increase of 9 per cent. in the first half of 1923 ; nothing so exceptional as to justify the High Commissioner's description of emergence from darkness to light.

Railway Direction. For the ten months of the Fascist regime the Italian railways had three heads : the Minister of Public Works, a lawyer; the High Commissioner, a medical man ; and the Director-General. Conflicts were continual, and finally the only technically competent head, SignorAlzona, the Director-General, resigned (August 2, 1923).

Leases to Private Industry. One of the fundamental points in the Fascist programme before Fascism came into power was the leasing of public services, and in particular railways, to private industry. Under-Secretary Rocco confirmed it on November 6, 1922 ; the Council of Ministers confirmed it, as regards the railways of the Trentino (frontier railways !) on November 14 ; and the Premier's Under-Secretary confirmed it on February 4, 1923, in the programme speech.

On March 15 the official Stefani agency announced that the Council of Ministers had approved the broad lines laid down in the report of the Minister of Public Works for the leasing of the State railways. "The complete transfer (*trapasso netto e preciso*) to private control is a political and economic necessity."

But four days later the High Commissioner corrected the report : "The scheme is merely one for the eventual leasing of the secondary lines." (March 19.)

An official communication on March 23 announced that the Council of Ministers had approved a contract for the leasing of certain lines to the Lombardy and Emilia Railway Company.

Next, on April 3, a Fascist, Signor Farinacci, of Cremona, intervened. The Commissioner, he said, and the Director-General of Railways knew nothing of the plans for leasing. ("Cremona Nuova," April 3.) And Mussolini telegraphed to Farinacci, April 4 : "I have given orders for the suspension of the execution of the agreement to lease railways of Cremona, despite the signature already affixed."

A final official communication announced on April 7 that the Council of Ministers had decided to "re-examine" the question and "co-ordinate it with the general plan of the leasing of the whole system."

And there the matter still rests !

VIII.—POSTAL AND ELECTRICAL SERVICES.

(1) The State telephone service had been bought at a fabulous ransom from private individuals who had been making a ruinous loss and had let the plant go to pieces. During the war the supply of fresh instruments had been suspended. After the war the service was reorganised, and 50,000 subscribers were transferred to an automatic exchange, furnished with instruments received from Germany on reparation account.

Under decree No. 399 of February 8, 1923, negotiations began for leasing the system to private enterprise, with the certainty that only the best services would be taken over, and the less remunerative zones left in the hands of the State—and even then indirect financing would be demanded from the State.

A decree was also published (No. 687, March 18) for the leasing of the telegraphs to private enterprise. Up to now, however, this has remained, fortunately, a mere paper project.

(2) Many employees on the postal accounting staff, especially women, who had served during and since the war, have been discharged for no other reason than to follow the current fashion, since numbers of them were re-engaged at lower rates of pay.

The Railway and Postal Accounts for 1922-23.

The Fascist press and Government claim to have made great savings in the postal and railway services. That may be so. But, once more, up to the present no official document has been issued to prove it.

Or, one—to support their hundred claims : it is contained in the Report of the Minister of Finances ; it is very summary ; and we reproduce it here.

Expenditure : (a) *Posts.* Ordinary expenditure, 1921-22, 752 million lire ; 1922-23, 809 millions ; an *increase.* Extraordinary, 1921-22, 385 millions ; 1922-23, 281 millions ; a *decrease,* but precisely in that part of the expenditure in which a saving is possible through reduced capital expenditure, using up stocks, and so on.

(b) *Railways* : Ordinary expenditure, 1921-22, 4,415 millions ; 1922-23, 4,206 millions, a *small reduction,* less than 5 per cent. As regards "general expenditure" there is an increase from 189 to 309 millions. Extraordinary expenditure, 1921-22, 502 millions ; 1922-23, 1,004 millions, *double* the preceding year— a figure capable of many interpretations, but quite different ones from the excuses of the Fascist press.

Revenue : (a) *Posts.* A normal increase, from 673 millions in 1921-22 to 734 millions in 1922-23.

(b) *Railways* : An increase, less than 5 per cent., from 3,157 millions in 1921-22 to 3,299 millions in 1922-23.

Nothing remarkable.

IX.—JUSTICE.

Amnesty? Under the decree of amnesty and pardon, No 1641 of December 22, 1922, full amnesty was granted for all crimes, without exception, even those carrying penal servitude (for example, homicide), to all those who had committed them for national (!) ends, even if only indirectly so, and even if not exclusively so but partly (though not predominantly) for personal ends (Article 1). On the first occasion of the application of this decree there were, among cases precisely similar as regards the crime committed, citizens fully amnestied (Fascists) and citizens refused any benefit from the decree, or allowed only one year's remission of sentence (non-Fascists).

As many criminal elements in the Fascist ranks had earlier convictions, the amnesty was extended even to habitual criminals or those with former convictions; exclusion from the benefit of the amnesty was confined to cases in which there were more than two convictions for the gravest crimes against persons or property. Not only that, but if the former convictions were for crimes committed "for national ends", there was no exclusion even in these cases (Article 7) ! Thus, considering that, of the tens of thousands of cases of violence, homicide, arson and intimidation of which Fascists had been guilty, only a fraction were denounced, and that of the few thousand cases denounced hardly more than a few hundreds of the gravest and most glaringly evident led to convictions, the amnesty ended in the absolution of all Fascist crimes, even the cruellest, the most horrible and most repugnant. Thus the amnesty was granted even to the persons charged with the assassination of the Deputy Di Vagno ; even to those guilty of theft and receiving (when the thief, being a Fascist, was able to give it to be understood that he had robbed in order to finance—the march on Rome!), and its application was allowed even for defamation and—adultery!

In contrast to this unheard-of generosity towards crimes committed for "national ends," the decree applied extreme severity to—the rest. The Premier wrote, in his letter of congratulation to the Minister, that through this provision the "so-called tyrannical Government was throwing open the prison gates," but the truth was that not a gate opened. For political or politically-inspired crimes (other than homicide) a year's remission was granted, and the same for those arising out of economic or social disturbances. Complete amnesty was granted only in cases of minor crimes, for which the minimum penalty does not exceed three years, and which were committed in connection with agitations, conflicts or disturbances with an economic or social origin. Hence the beneficiaries were *extremely few.*

The decree of April 9, 1923, simply granted a remission of three months for common crimes; a grotesque and unjust provision.

The most recent decree, of October 31, 1923, granted amnesty for politically-inspired crimes, but excluded all crimes against the security of the State and those for which the minimum penalty exceeds three years. In the latter case a few years' remission was allowed in consideration of certain extenuating circumstances, but never in the case of crimes against the security of the State.

A true amnesty, a true pacification should have applied precisely to the crimes against the person committed during the virtual civil war of 1921 and 1922, crimes dealt with by juries which frequently were bound to be led astray by hate or terror. For every Fascist loss in that period, the arm of the law was invoked against dozens of "subversives"; and the heaviest sentences were inflicted, *with or without proof of guilt*, often with doctored evidence, and above all without the least consideration for the conditions of suggestion and environment which modified the criminality of the offence committed.[1]

Precisely these cases have been excluded from all benefit from the amnesty. Mercy and justice have thus been converted into a party weapon.

[1] In the Province of Bologna alone, in seventeen prosecutions of so-called "subversives," sentences totalling 1,125 years of penal servitude were inflicted. In the Assizes at Trani, in two single prosecutions, 700 years of imprisonment were inflicted on 40 peasants.

X.—SCHOOLS.

The decrees promulgated by the Fascist Minister of Education, profiting by the plenary powers of the Government, have thrown the educational system of the country into confusion.

Universities. There were too many Italian Universities—seventeen—and they were insufficiently financed.[1] The new Government added two new ones (Milan and Bari), augmented the faculties of others, increasing the existing duplication, and is reducing the financial support accorded, which is already insufficient in several cases.

As to organisation, the universities are becoming free —to seek means of existence; but they are losing the right to elect their Rectors, governing bodies and Pro-

[1] On June 14, 1922, the Chamber of Deputies adopted the following resolution, moved by the Socialist group:

"The Chamber invites the Government to take steps for the reorganisation of the numerous Italian universities, reducing to the indispensable minimum the number of complete universities and converting the smaller ones into specialised institutions, so permitting more serious organisation and better endowment."

fessors, which is being largely assumed by the Government. Their curricula are still drawn up by the Faculties, but have to receive the approval of the Superior Council of Public Instruction, which is entirely nominated by the Minister. Finally the Minister has instituted an internal university police (legalised espionage?), formed from among the subordinate civil servants and the ushers. (Royal decree No. 2102, September 30, 1923.)

The *Secondary Schools* have been deliberately transformed with a view to keeping away from them as many pupils as possible and diverting pupils to the private schools, even if there is a deficiency of the latter or they are less efficient than the State schools. (Royal decree No. 1054, May 6, 1923.)

The first steps taken by the Ministry resulted in the refusal of facilities for admission to the Secondary Schools to some 50,000 candidates. This aroused a revolt in the Press and among the students' families, and was modified in some degree by combining courses (Royal decree No. 2370, October 15, 1923), raising the class numbers to 40, and other similar devices; even so the Minister has had to confess that 18,301 students have failed to gain admission, not through failure to come up to the educational standard, but through local deficiencies; in the smaller centres and in various districts, by the Minister's own admission, the public Secondary Schools have 65,607 vacancies! So enormous are the miscalculations and failures of organisation in his reform.

The new Girls' Lyceums, intended for the middle class only, have enrolled absurdly small numbers of students; as to the new Complementary Schools, for the proletariat, parents refused to send their children to them as they were first planned. Meanwhile, nothing has been done for the Technical Schools, some of which have been suppressed. Heaviest of all is the blow aimed at the Normal Schools (for teachers in the Elementary Schools), which have been cut down from 153 to 87. (Article 58 of Royal decree No. 1054, May 6, 1923.)

Primary Schools. On November 14, 1922, the promise was made of "the spread of popular education," and on May 1, 1923, the Fascist Government published the decree authorising the 6,000 new schools already proposed by the Socialist group, in face of an illiteracy in Italy which still exceeds 30 per cent. Now, however, the Minister declares that there are 10,000 inefficient schools (whose is the responsibility?), and as a first step he is turning over 3,000 schools to the Committee for Combating Illiteracy, which will place them out by contract under ill-paid or unqualified masters. (Royal decree No. 2410, October 31, 1923.)

The intention has also been announced of entrusting schools to private individuals, simply granting a subsidy (Royal decree No. 2410 of October 26, 1923) ; and preparations are being made for the return of the schools to the Communes, with the system of State contributions which has already shown its complete bankruptcy precisely in the less developed districts, in which the need of schools was greatest.

With the imposition of religious (Catholic) instruction in the Elementary Schools [1] (Royal decree No. 2185, October 1, 1923), and of a State philosophy in the Secondary Schools (Royal decree No. 2345, October 14), and with the political oath imposed on all teachers, even in the Universities, the educational system has completely lost its lay quality. (Royal decree No. 2102, September 30, 1923.)

With the abolition of all elected representative bodies, and the loss of all judicial guarantees, the teachers' organisations have been rendered valueless; and all, after thirty years of struggle, have been sub-

jected to the arbitrary control of the central power, and
so of the Government bureaucracy and the Minister.

[1] Article 3 of the decree of October 1 reads as follows: "The
basis and the crown of every grade of elementary instruction must
be instruction in the Christian doctrine according to the form
which it has received in the Catholic tradition. In judging the
aptitude of teachers and other persons for imparting religious
instruction, the *Regio Provedditore agli Studi* will conform to the
views of the competent ecclesiastical authority."
The following was the opinion of Signor Gentile, the Fascist
Minister of Education, before the coming of Fascism:
"The school is, or should be, the place of instruction in a
common truth and a common justice for all; by its very nature it
should instil fraternity and unity and gentleness. . . . Denominational instruction, on the contrary, coarsens the spirit, investing
it with a new insensitiveness (*durezza*) . . . it destroys the
innate faith in the unity of the true and the good, and splits up
the human race in the student's view into two parts, the elect
and the reprobate. . . . In place of fraternity, division; in
place of collaboration, intolerance! . . .
"It produces another defect yet graver than intolerance: the
instinctive resistance to the free development of scientific thought
in the broadest sense. . . .
"And a yet deeper and more radical fault is that it tends to rob
the spirit of the sense of its own self-mastery, and so of its own
responsibility, not only moral but intellectual. . . .
"Thus the denominational school is not a school but the negation
of a school." (Report to 1907 Congress, in "Education and the
Lay School," Florence, 1922.)

XI.—THE OCCUPATION OF CORFU.

"If Greece does not pay, I shall remain for an in-
definite period in possession of Corfu, which for
centuries was uninterruptedly Venetian territory."
(Mussolini, in interview with the London "Daily Mail,"
September 4, 1923.)

"Should the League of Nations declare its com-
petence in the matter, the question will arise for Italy
whether to remain in the League of Nations or to leave
it. I have already decided for the second course in that
eventuality." (Mussolini, official communication,
September, 4, 1923.)

"The action taken does not exclude the sanctions
which the Conference of Ambassadors may take."

(Mussolini, circular to Italy's representatives abroad. Rome, August 31, 1923.)

"In the circular issued to-day Signor Mussolini makes a clear distinction : there are the reparations due to Italy and those due to the Conference of Ambassadors. The Premier cannot agree to the substitution of an assembly of which Italy forms only a part, for Italy herself, in making the demand for the reparations which are expected for Italy. The massacre of the Italian mission is a blow primarily at Italy and only secondarily at the other Powers. . . . Signor Mussolini declares that the one action does not exclude the other, but that the two must not be confused or superposed." (Semi-official comment, August 31.)

At Paris, on September 27, the Conference of Ambassadors imposed on Greece the payment of 50 million lire to Italy. The Italian troops evacuated Corfu. But the assassins who killed the Italian mission still remained unpunished.

At Geneva, on September 28, Viscount Ishii, the President of the Council, said that "the members of the Council of the League of Nations are in agreement in recognising that every controversy between members of the League which is susceptible of producing a rupture, comes within the sphere of activity of the League, and that if such controversy proves incapable of regulation either through diplomatic channels or by arbitral procedure or under a judicial decision, it is the duty of the Council to take cognisance of the matter, within the limits óf Article 15 of the Pact."

The occupation of Corfu procured no benefit for Italy ; still less did her unworthy treatment of the League of Nations.

Much more fruitful and valuable will be her policy of agreement with Jugoslavia concerning Fiume, which was advocated all along by the reviled "renunciators" and fiercely obstructed by all the Nationalists, among them Signor Mussolini, who, for instance, defined the port arrangement and the cession of Porto Baros to Jugoslavia as "a diabolical plan" and "the ruin of Fiume."

XII.—A Party Police.

Strength. Before the war, the Italian police force consisted of 28,100 carabineers, and 10,400 gendarmes, a total of 38,500. After the war there was created the Guardia Regia ("Royal Guards"), with an initial strength of 25,000 men, subsequently increased. All the parliamentary reports demanded the unification of the police forces, their diminution in strength, and their improvement in quality.

The Fascist Government had no liking for the Guardia Regia, and abolished it accordingly—not without disturbances, revolts, and executions; but the carabineers, of whom Mussolini has publicly stated that they were friendly to the Fascists even before the arrival of the latter in power, have been increased in strength to 78,000 (now to be reduced to 67,000); and there has been instituted the National Militia of the first proclamation, 200,000 strong, with no sort of legal or parliamentary authority; a total of 278,000 men.

Functions and Selection. Mussolini's Under-Secretary declared in his programme speech of February 4, 1923, that the Guardia Regia had been abolished as "its primary function was the purely factious one of supporting the party in power."

However, under the decrees of January 14, 1923, and later dates, the new Fascist Government instituted a definitely political police "under the orders of the Premier," and enrolled exclusively "through the organisation of the Fascist party" (declaration of General De Bono).

The National Militia is composed entirely of Fascists, enrolled under various proclamations. The Grand

Fascist Council has declared that it is composed of 200,000 under the first proclamation and 100,000 under the second; clearly without any selection but that of party. Ex-lieutenants of the army have been able to jump suddenly up to militia ranks equivalent to those of Colonel or General, with pay in proportion.

The expenditure on the Militia in the first six months of 1923 was 47 million lire; and it made use of a large part of the barrack buildings and supplies belonging to the Guardia Regia. For 1923-24 25 millions has been provided.

The Fascist Militia enjoys special reductions of railway fares. (Decree No. 816, March 18, 1923.) Unlimited provision is made for its equipment, and expenditure thereon does not require the assent of the Council of State. (Decree No. 467, February 25, 1923.)

Decree No. 2146, September 26, 1923, lays down that officers and State employees permanently employed in the National Militia are to receive in addition to their ordinary pay a monthly allowance of 150 to 500 lire.

Militiamen are often employed in attendance on private companies, and in such cases they remain there even if called out for service (Decree No. 1880, August 20, 1923); in various tramway and similar undertakings they also receive pay from the firm.

All militiamen, that is all Fascists, may carry revolvers, even when off duty, and are exempt from payment for licence. (Decree No. 1881, August 20.) On the other hand, the Prefects have issued orders that all "subversives," that is all non-Fascists, are prohibited from carrying arms.

The Militia serves purely political purposes; "The Militia is a great political police force; its duty is to render impossible any disturbance of the public order, any gesture or attempt at sedition against the Fascist

Government." (Grand Fascist Council, July 25, 1923.) The Commandant, General De Bono, sends out public telegrams declaring his readiness "to kill" (whom? Italian citizens?) "for Fascism." (November 23, 1923.)

Italy is the only civilised country in which a party militia is kept under arms, and paid at the expense of the State, against another part of the citizens.

XIII.—THE STATE ENSLAVED BY A PARTY.

The Fascist Militia, paid out of the revenue of the State, has been substituted for a police force impartially recruited from among all the citizens, in violation of Article 24 of the Constitution, under which "all citizens are equally admissible to civil and military posts."

The Grand Fascist Council has taken the place of the Council of Ministers in disposing of the affairs of the nation.

On October 9, 1923, the Executive of the Fascist party declared that any form of interference on the part of representatives of the party with the organs of the Government was prohibited; but at the same time it was continually calling for reports from Prefects of the Italian State (for example, at Girgenti, Trapani, Pesaro, Grosseto, etc.), and giving them instructions or orders.[1]

[1] Here is one of the most curious of these orders. The Secretariat of the Fascist party sent to the Provincial Fascist Federations and the *Prefects* of the Kingdom the following circular :

"The National Directory desires that virtually all the Fasci should resume their social duties towards the electoral system, so that there may be guaranteed to every current of opinion the right to express its own ideas and, by means of the vote, to express its wishes. In this way the National Directory counts on providing an outlet (*dare sfogo*) for all the passions which hitherto have disturbed the internal unity of the various Fasci. . . . It is not intended, however, that the meetings of the Fasci should be transformed into battlefields between rival Fascists.

At Palermo all the Prefects of Sicily were summoned to a meeting under the presidency of Signor Terruzzi, who holds no State appointment whatever, but is merely a member of the executive committee of the Fascist party.

The Prefects, police superintendents and commandants of carabineers have always, in every important question, to consult the leader of the local Fascio.

Some Prefects actually take part in Fascist public demonstrations against other parties (for example, the Prefect of Trapani on October 4, 1923).

October 28 to 30 was celebrated as a national festival in commemoration of the violent conquest of power by the Fascists. Even the King took part in it.

The Fascist trade union federations issue proclamations such as this :

"It has been ascertained that the rural workers are forming armed bands directed against the Fascist trade unionists, and that the authority of the Prefect no

"You are accordingly to adopt the following measures :

"Both at meetings of the Fasci for the nomination of Political Secretaries, and in the meetings of Provincial Councils for nominations to the Federations and nominations of Provincial Secretaries, there is to be allowed the fullest liberty of discussion. The discussion is to take place under the forms of procedure dictated by the most elementary sense of civil and political education. No violence of any sort is to be allowed ; Fascists are to be prevented from bringing arms into the meeting. Fascists already expelled who try to re-enter the meeting hall will immediately be arrested by the National Militia and the Carabineers.

"The chairman of the meeting will have at his disposition within the hall the senior commanding officer of the Militia, to whom he will give necessary instructions for the maintenance of internal order.

"Outside the hall there will be a delegate of the police, with a detachment of Royal Carabineers.

"If serious disturbances should break out at any time, the police authority will be authorised to break up the meeting, occupy the hall and detain the Fascio.

"All those within the hall who prove to have been provoking disturbances or violence may be arrested." (November, 1923.)

longer prevails. . . . Those present accordingly declare that they are forming themselves into a secret local committee of defence, directly responsible to the General Secretariat of the Fascist trade union federation of Padua.'' (Padua, August 15, 1923.)

The Ministers of the Navy and of War invited holders of the gold medal (for valour at the Front) to take part in the Fascist anniversary celebrations, and authorised them to recover their travelling expenses from the headquarters of the Fascist party (October 21, 1923).

At Naples the Executive of the Italian Nationalist Association issued this communication :

''In view of the particularly grave situation in those provinces in which, as at Naples, the authorities have openly assisted the Fascist efforts to gain control of affairs by force, to the injury of the Nationalist groups. . . .'' (December 30, 1922.)

''At Turin,'' wrote the *Popolo d'Italia*[1] itself, ''there was no sign either of the Prefect or of the Superintendent of Police ; accordingly the police took no action, and completely abdicated its functions in favour of the *squadre d'azione*'' (armed Fascist bands). (December 28, 1922.)

Things have gone so far that the Fascist Federation of the Polesine (delta of the Po) issued the following circular :

''With a view to giving the Federation a system of administration . . . the Council proposes to assess contributions on the basis of the Government assessments of income and taxation, and to require the tax-collectors to collect them. Signed : Luigi Arcangeli, Enzo Casalini.'' (Rovigo, April 2, 1923.)

By an abuse of the plenary powers law (which was intended to *simplify* administration), the Government

[1] Mussolini's organ.—*Trans.*

has decreed the issue of a special series of postage stamps, bearing, instead of the emblems of the Italian State and monarchy, those of the Fascist party. (Decree No. 3451, October 21, 1923.) So also for small coin.

All Fascists or persons in the favour of the Fascists may carry revolvers, and no one else. (Circular of the Prefect of Novara.)

The Fascist button is virtually an indispensable condition for freedom from molestation in the public services. Numberless State employees, professors, magistrates and workers have been required to resign or dismissed, for the single reason that they were not in the good graces of the Fascist party. In the lower grades discharges have been made by the thousand. In the higher grades there have occurred the unheard-of cases of the retirement on pension of the senior President of the Supreme Court, Ludovico Mortara, who had been a member of a former Ministry; and the dismissal of Professor Lombardo Pellegrino, a Deputy belonging to the Constitutional opposition party, without prior notice!

To sum up, *membership of the Fascist party is a second and more important form of Italian citizenship; to be without it is to forego civil rights, and to lose liberty of voting, domicile, movement, assembly, work, speech, and even thought.*

XIV.—ELECTORATE AND ELECTIONS.

On November 14, 1922, Signor Mussolini declared to the Paris "Journal," "I shall not give women the vote. It is useless. In Germany and England the women voters vote for men."

But in 1923 the Fascist Government proposed to give women the municipal vote. This, however, it made a privilege of certain categories, the most numerous being that of the possessors of an educational certificate, such as working-class women usually do not possess, and that of the owners of property of a certain value.

Thus the ostensible concession of women's suffrage is in reality a step away from universal suffrage, and a return to plural votes for the propertied class as against the single vote of the proletarian.

The new law governing Parliamentary elections is so framed as to give the Government party 356 seats in Parliament out of the total of 535, even if it obtains no more than a quarter of the votes cast. The list of the 356 Deputies of the majority is determined, name by name, by the Prime Minister of the Government in power. The minority parties may only divide among themselves 179 seats in Parliament, even if they gain together more than half the votes cast.

The Italian municipal elections of 1923 took place virtually everywhere amid violence and intimidation. Before and during the elections the Fascist Militia was mobilized and fully armed. As a rule the Opposition parties were unable even to present their lists of candidates, and in many hundreds of Communes the Fascists ran both majority and minority candidates. This is a sample Fascist electoral manifesto :

A CHI NON VOTA

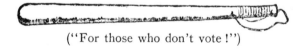

("For those who don't vote !")

XV.—THE MUTILATION OF THE LOCAL AUTHORITIES.

In Italy, especially Northern Italy, the Commune has a long history of achievement. In the New Provinces won from Austria the decentralised local administration had given remarkable results in simplicity and rapidity of functioning. The islands and Southern Italy had demanded similar autonomy, especially in regard to public works.

The Fascist Government, on the contrary, is destroying all local autonomy, centralising everything in the hands either of the Government at Rome or of the Prefects or Vice-Prefects.

The reform of the legislation affecting Communes and Provinces, announced and so often described in semi-official communications, has, fortunately, not yet been initiated. Nevertheless, and despite the declaration of the head of the Government on October 8, 1923, that "the Government has no intention of placing the Communes in tutelage or taking away from them the administrative autonomy which is essential to them," a series of steps have been taken which have played havoc with the local authorities.

(a) *Communal and Provincial Administrations Dissolved.* Several hundred Communal administrations had been dissolved up to October 31, 1923, including those of Belluno, Vicenza, Verona, Treviso, Pavia, Catania, Benevento, Lecce, Como, Messina, Avellino, Syracuse, Bari, Trapani, Trento, Bergamo, and Rome.

The Provincial Councils of Florence, Pavia, and Novara were dissolved in November, 1922; Siena, Reggio Emilia, Belluno, Cremona, Milan, and Ancona in December; Syracuse, Foggia, Girgenti, Verona, Venice, and Como in January, 1923; Trieste, Udine, Potenza, Benevento, Parma, and Treviso in March; Caltanissetta in April; Rome in May; Zara in May; Bergamo in July; Teramo, Cagliari and Reggio Calabria in August; Macerata and Trento in September; Catania and Messina in October.

These are the dissolutions publicly announced, and the list is not complete. The public announcements are always in arrear, frequently by four or five months, in violation of the Royal decree, which provided for immediate publication in the Official Gazette.

Article 323 of the Law concerning Communes and Provinces lays down that the Government is to communicate a list of Communes dissolved every three months to the Senate and the Chamber, in order that they may have some control over the process. Instead of this, the Government communicated in November the list of Councils closed between January and April, and there is no official knowledge of what has happened since !

Apart from formal dissolution, there have been innumerable virtual dissolutions through the appointment of prefectoral Commissioners. When asked as to the number of these, the Minister *refused to reply;* so concealing an illegal state of affairs, since the law permits dissolution only for definite practical reasons.

The law requires that within three months of the dissolution of a Commune fresh elections shall be held; only in exceptional cases is a period of six months allowed.

Under the Fascist Government the exceptional has become the normal. Prorogations for six months have become habitual, and, in open violation of the law, have reached a year and more; in Rome a Royal Commissioner has been placed in control for 22 months !

(b) *Reasons for Dissolution.* The law allows the dissolution of Councils only for grave reasons of public order, or for violation of the law. The Fascist Government is dissolving Councils simply because they are not Fascist, or are obnoxious to local Fascists. And public order is being protected not by the punishment of armed assault or intimidation of the municipal bodies, but by pursuing the legitimate administrators if they show resistance. Here are a few typical instances of the reasons advanced in the decrees dissolving Communes :

64

Bertinoro (Forlo) : "In consequence of political events and of the changed attitude of public opinion, and of the occupation of the town hall." (Decree of January 8, 1923.)

Reggio Emilia : "In consequence of past and recent resignations, in the existing condition of public feeling, which continues to be agitated by party conflicts." (Decree of September 2, 1923.)

Sesto S. Giovanni (Milan) : "Following the occupation of the town hall on October 31 by elements opposed to the administration . . . and on account of irregular and partial action, particularly in the distribution of the principal duties, and of the public funds, and of dissatisfaction arising therefrom." (Decree of September 13, 1923.)

Parabiago (Milan) : "On account of the occupation of the town hall on the night of November 1 by opponents of the administration, and the consequent resignation of 15 out of the 20 legally appointed councillors." (Decree of February 16.)

Biancavilla (Catania) : "On account of the dissensions among local parties, the misgovernment by the administration, which did not respect the will of the majority, provoking a movement of reaction which culminated in the violent occupation of the offices. It is to be feared that the convocation of the Council might provoke conflicts." (Decree of March 6, 1923.)

Busto Arsizio (Milan) : "For having acted under the inspiration of party aims, provoking lively opposition and ultimately the invasion of the town hall." (Decree of April 10.)

Castelfiume (Aquila) : "Other irregularities, and finally grave reasons of public order, provoked demonstrations which culminated on November 21 in the invasion of the town hall." (Decree of April 10.)

Pozzuoli (Naples) : "Owing to bad administration

and acts of favouritism, there was evidence of grave discontent with the administrators, which was accentuated after recent political events, and produced in the Commune an extremely grave and alarming situation, as is shown by the manifestation during which the Communal buildings were occupied." (Decree of July 7.)

Levico (Trento) : "Because in resisting the action of the political authorities it was constantly inspired by anti-national sentiments." (Decree of August 20.)

S. Dorriigo della Valle (Trento) : "The administrators having pursued anti-national propaganda, obstructing the work of the political authorities." (Decree of September 2.)

S. Domenica Vittoria (Messina) : "Owing to the loss of the support of public opinion, which had changed in the direction of the new national political currents." (Decree of September 10.)

Ali Marina (Messina) : "Owing to the profound change evidenced in the political views of the population, following recent national events." (Decree of October 21, 1923.)

Frattamaggiore (Naples) : "Owing to the attitude taken up by the local administration, which isolated itself from the national political currents, and initiated against its opponents a whole system of persecutions and reprisals, which produced strong excitement among the greater part of the population." (Decree of November 15, 1923.)

Rome : *"For the calm and objective study of the conditions of the Commune* of Rome, it appears necessary to eliminate the existing elected administration, which, for the rest, was in a critical situation." (Semi-official communication of March 1, 1923.)

And nine months later : "The Council of Ministers confirms the continuation for a further 12 months of the powers of the Commissioner of Rome." (Semi-official communication of November 30, 1923.)

And, as a last manifestation of the respect of the Government for the autonomy of the local administrations, under

Decree of September 24, 1923 : "In substitution for Article 324 of the Law concerning the Municipalities, the Government has been empowered to confer on the Commissioners and Commissions of Communes and Provinces the powers of the respective Councils" !

(c) *Joint Administrative Areas.* The Fascist executive power has even interfered with the joint administrative areas (*Circoscrizioni locali*), in contravention of Article 74 of the Constitution and articles 118 and onwards of the Law concerning Communes and Provinces.

At Milan the head of the Government, Signor Mussolini, intervened personally to impose the aggregation of 11 neighbouring Communes, without any request from the administrations concerned, and increased the communal councillors from 80 to 91, the additional 11 councillors being nominated by Royal decree ! (Royal decree No. 1912, September 2, 1923.)

At Portomaurizio and Oneglia, while four Communes had been discussing amalgamation, the Royal decree No. 3360 of October 21, 1923, imposed the amalgamation of 14 Communes; a further 90 Communes were reduced by amalgamations to 25 as a result of deliberations of—the Council of Ministers.

At Massa and Lucca, Government decrees ordered partitions which threw the population into confusion, and set the Fascists of the two Provinces against one another.

Appropriation of Local Profits. Under Royal decree No. 477, of May 18, 1923, the savings and profits made by local associations out of purchases of supplies were *appropriated to the State.*

(d) *Autonomy of Minority Populations.* Respect for the autonomous local authorities of the New Provinces was assumed everywhere by both the letter and the spirit of the Treaty of St. Germain, and was formally promised in the decree of annexation. Above all, it was explicitly required by the Law No. 1322 of September 26, 1920, which embodied the Royal decree No. 1804 of October 6, 1919. Article 4 of this law, in authorising the Government to publish in the annexed territories the Italian Constitution and the rest of the Italian laws, and to co-ordinate them with the legislation in force in these territories, added : *"in particular with their provincial and communal autonomy."*

The central and regional consultative committees, which contained representatives of the localities concerned in the New Provinces, directly appointed, and selected without distinction of political party, had also performed their duty in pronouncing in favour of the maintenance of the autonomous Provincial and Communal administrations. But the Fascist Government dissolved these committees and instituted fresh consultative committees, of which one-half consisted of political representatives of the New Provinces and the other half of members nominated by the Prime Minister. (Royal decree No. 1446, November 16, 1922.)

Then, in direct contravention of Article 4 of the Law of September 26, 1920, and of the vote of the direct representatives of the New Provinces, Royal decree No. 9 of January 11, 1923, extended to the annexed territories the Italian Communal and Provincial law, and the regulations thereunder, with a few immaterial alterations.

So was ended the promised autonomy of the New Provinces, and the hope of all who had sought to learn, from the simpler Austrian system, improvements which could be introduced in Italy.

On the other hand, even the Italian system has not actually been introduced, since, under decree of March 22, 1923, the administrative elections in the New Provinces were postponed; and the system of Royal Commissioners is still in full force.

XVI.—Constitution, Propaganda, etc.

Commendatore Michele Bianchi, as Secretary of the Fascist party, announced that after the elections the Fascist Government would propose a reform of the Constitution on the lines of the Prussian Chancellorship:

"As soon as the King, after the elections, has entrusted the formation of the Government to the politician most in tune with the will of the nation, and as soon as this man has announced his programme in the Chamber and the Chamber has approved it, the Government shall have no need during its term of office of any further vote of confidence." (Speech at Milan, March 26, 1923.)

An Under-Secretary of State has stated that the Fascist leaders are pestering the King to make this change in the Constitution, and hope to succeed.

In various Ministries there have been instituted Press Bureaux, responsible for securing publicity for every smallest action of the Fascist Government; and there has been instituted abroad an intensive campaign of Fascist propaganda, which is certainly not the same thing as a propaganda purely in the national interests.

Meanwhile, at the expense of every Italian citizen, there has been incurred the following expenditure, outside the sums already provided in the budget:

Decree dated 1922	No.	Head of expenditure	Lire
Dec. 7 ...	1633	Prime Minister's Press Bureau...	50,000
1923 Feb. 8 ...	288	Incidental, Prime Minister's Office	120,000
Feb. 8 ...	289	Prime Minister's Press Bureau...	25,000
Mar. 11 ...	661	Incidental, Prime Minister's Office	150,000
Mar. 25 ...	1017	Highway Robbery in Sicily ...	1,000,000
Mar. 25 ...	774	Secret international expenditure	2,673,500
April 19 ...	891	Secret, for National Militia ...	300,000
April 19 ...	829	Incidental, Prime Minister's Office	40,000
April 26 ...	1171	Press Bureau, Ministry of the Interior	50,000
June 14 ...	1320	Incidental, Prime Minister's Office	150,000
June 28 ...	1589	Prime Minister's Office	191,000
June 12 ...	1602	Police duties abroad ...	350,000
Sept. 10 ...	1967	Foreign Ministry, missions ...	20,000
Sept. 10 ...	1967	Secret Service, Ministry of the Interior	800,000
Sept. 15 ...	2061	Secret expenditure, propaganda abroad	1,000,000
Sept. 24 ...	2033	Contingent expenditure abroad...	25,000
Sept. 24 ...	2033	Prime Minister's Press Bureau	95,000
Oct. 21 ...	2301	Foreign Ministry, missions ...	24,000
Oct. 21 ...	2301	Incidental, Prime Minister's Office	15,000
Oct. 21 ...	2302	Incidental, Prime Minister's Office	100,000
Oct. 7 ...	2190	Secret expenditure abroad ...	4,600,000
Specification	107	Ministry of the Interior, secret expenditure, National Militia...	600,000

Tuberculosis. Such legislation or fragmentary provisions as former Governments had initiated, have been left unapplied. The new Prefects are advising against the application even of existing legislation requiring local committees to be set up, and these have scarcely been instituted in a single province.

Alcoholism. On September 12, 1923, an official communication was issued announcing that, in order to combat alcoholism, the Council of Ministers had approved a decree "fixing the closing hour for licensed houses at 10 p.m. in winter and 11 p.m. in summer, and the opening hour at 10 a.m."

The publicans complained and agitated.

On October 23 a circular was issued which virtually annulled the decree, "delegating to the Prefects of the various Provinces the decision as to variations of the closing hour, account being taken of the importance of the town concerned and the movement of visitors."

Gambling. On November 29, 1922, the Under-Secretary for the Interior stated in the Senate that "It is impossible to prevent gambling. . . . The question of granting licenses to gaming houses is under consideration. . . . The plan to be submitted for the King's approval is at the present moment under consideration."

Two months later, the semi-official press reported that the intention of the Government was the precise opposite of that already announced, and that all gambling would be prohibited.

Letters of Introduction. At the end of 1922 the Ministers sent to all Deputies a circular asking them to desist from putting forward any sort of request for favours for private individuals.

After less than a year, letters of recommendation and replies to them were in full flow once more, though restricted to certain Deputies; and communications of the type of the following were being issued :

"August 29, 1923. The press bureau of the Fascist party of Aquila reports that 'in consequence of the great interest shown by His Excellency Alessandro Sardi, Signor Mussolini has arranged for the suspension of the order for the dismantling of the workshops attached to the boot and shoe works at Aquila, which have already been closed down.' "

PART III.

THE WORDS OF THE LEADERS—
1922.

November 11. "If the dictatorship has not been installed, the Chamber is begged to harbour no illusions. If it does any mischief it will be suppressed." *Popolo d'Italia* (Mussolini's paper).

November 17. "With 300,000 men fully armed, absolutely determined, and almost mystically eager to obey my command, I shall be able to punish all who have abused and attempted to besmirch Fascism.

"I could have made of this grey and frigid hall a cohort's bivouac; I could have shut up Parliament and constituted a Government exclusively of Fascists. I could have done so, but I did not desire to, at all events in these first days. . . .

"So far as it is possible for me to avoid it, I do not want to govern against the Chamber; but the Chamber must realise its situation, which renders it liable to be dissolved at any time, the day after to-morrow or in two years' time." *Mussolini*, in the Chamber.

December 8. "Our propaganda will be Fascism, Fascism and Fascism; and for those who are hard of hearing we announce that the *manganello* (bludgeon) will be able to work wonders." *Bolzoni,* of the Fascist Party executive, in an interview.

December 19. "The wounding of the Fascist Boretti the other evening at Campi Bisenzio has given occasion for various reprisals. Some Florentine Fascists joined those of the locality and went to the quarter of S. Martino, where Serelli, the Socialist ex-syndic, was living; they made him sign a declaration binding himself to leave the district within forty-eight hours, and then constrained him to administer to himself a moderate dose of castor oil. Then they got on the track of excouncillor Nesti, and imposed on him an identical declaration and an equal dose of castor oil.   There remained the rector of Capolle, against whom the Fascists had already directed preliminary reprisals, which had their epilogue about 10 p.m. with a large glassful of castor oil.   On their way back the Fascists fell in with the Communist Vittorio Ballerini, who came to words with them but had the worst of the encounter, since he remained behind with a few bumps on the head." *Popolo d'Italia.* (Mussolini's paper.)

December 12. "We should like to have kissed on their sunlit brow those youngsters who stood on the outskirts of the town, stopped the citizens on their way out, and asked them if they had voted, making them go back if they could not give this assurance. . . Even if some of the young innocents were cheekily parading in their girdles a big revolver or a little stiletto." (Milan local elections.) *Popolo d'Italia.* (Mussolini's paper.)

December 12. "Certain Chairmen of Councils who were over-pedantic or over-partisan have received certain efficacious correctives from the Fascists." *Popolo d'Italia.* (Mussolini's paper.)

December 15. "Certain tiny minorities of ignorant politicians who have not yet given up the battle have been trying to profit by my short absence. . . . In any case, I ask the Council of Ministers to authorise me, from this moment onwards, to use whatever means seem to me most convenient against anyone, of whatever party, faction or sect, who attempts to produce disturbance or disorder in the country." *Mussolini,* speech to the Council of Ministers.

December 15. "The Fascist Government cannot tolerate these attempts at resuming the offensive on any side, and where they do not immediately cease it may be reduced to the hard but inexorable necessity of repressing them quickly and vigorously. . . . This does not mean that it is only for them (the Communists) that this lack of understanding may have tragic consequences. If in other camps, which the country has not been accustomed to regard as subversive, there are persons who are organising obscure and ambiguous movements, it is well to let them know that they must desist.'' *Mussolini*, speech to the Council of Ministers.

* * * * *

1923.

February 11. "The Prime Minister said to me one day that if the Fascists want the death penalty instituted, we can allow it, but from now onwards killing must be done in the name of the law and of the State. . . . If, however, the forces of opposition continued their harmful activities, some of the *piazze* (market places) of Italy would soon see the arrival of execution squads." Interview with *Giunta*, secretary of the Fascist party.

February 11. "In internal politics there is nothing to discuss; what is happening is happening by my precise and direct will and under my orders, for which, naturally, I assume full personal responsibility. . . And those who may intend to defame (Fascism) abroad and threaten it at home, must understand that their action entails possible consequences of the harshest. The enemies of the Fascist State must not be surprised if I treat them, as such, with severity. . . ." *Mussolini*, speech in the Chamber.

February 20. "I do not repent of my action in raising my revolver in the Chamber. . . . We have not formed the National Militia for nothing. If these forces of opposition are to spread, we shall plant execution squads in the *piazze* of Italy." *Giunta*, speech at Trieste.

February 13. "Communists have been arrested by thousands, and the reason is that we have no love for half-measures. . . . Where they prove to be innocent we shall release them at once. . . . in the Marches we have released 200 who had been arrested as a precautionary measure. But we shall keep in gaol those who are a danger to the State. As to the plot, we can say nothing at present" (*and nothing was ever discovered!*). *Finzi*, Under-Secretary in the Ministry of the Interior, in an interview.

March. "In Russia and in Italy it has been proved that it is possible to govern outside, above and against all Liberal ideology. . . .

"It may be taken as axiomatic that any sort of Government action provokes discontents. How will you avoid the growth of this discontent into a flood which constitutes a danger to the solidity of the State? You will avoid it by means of force, by accumulating the maximum of force. By making use of this force, inexorably, when it proves necessary. . . . Now, Fascism throws on the rubbish heap all these anti-vital theories. When a group or a party is in power, it is its duty to fortify its position and to defend itself against all comers. . . . Men are, perhaps, tired of Liberty.

"Let it be realised, then, once for all, that Fascism recognises no idols, adores no fetishes; it has already passed, and, if necessary, it will turn again and pass once more, over the more or less decomposed body of the Goddess of Liberty." *Mussolini, in Gerarchia.*

March 7. "Some may ask, why all this shouting and arming?

"I declare that I wish to govern, if possible, with the consent of the majority of the citizens; but while we are waiting for this consent to develop and feed and grow strong, I am accumulating the maximum of obtainable force.

"For it is possible that force may induce a discovery of consent, and in any case where consent is lacking there is still force." *Mussolini*, speech in the Ministry of Finances.

March 4. "The emissaries of Moscow and their worthy companions must understand at last that the times have changed. Otherwise they will be made to learn it by those who have the right and the duty to make them, and it will be a painful experience." *Popolo d'Italia*.

*   *   *   *   *

June 21. "When the head of the Government sends out his appeal, '*A noi* !' ('Up, and at them !'), the people will assist the Black Shirts [1] in overturning every obstacle in the way of the consummation of the revolution." *Popolo d'Italia*.

June 9. "But if the enemy raise their heads again, and make their more or less stupid opposition heard, the Fascists will close ranks once more; and then, woe to the vanquished! . . . The dominant feature of those two years, 1921 and 1922, was the succession of Fascist punitive expeditions. The necessity of the case drove the Fascists to proceed to the assault of the towns in vast armed masses. . . . The measures adopted for the restoration of public order are: first of all, the raking in of the so-called *sovversivi* ("subversives"). . . . It has been quite a modest affair: two thousand arrested; 150 are still in prison. They were elements of disorder and subversivism. It may be that Liberal practice would permit these elements to be allowed a free hand, but I am not inclined to follow that practice. . . ." *Mussolini*, speech in the Senate.

June 19. "Let no one abuse our spirit of generosity; otherwise force will be resorted to. If those residual elements of whom I spoke . . . should have any

[1] That is, the Fascists.

intention of still playing some part on the political stage, they know, and all Italians should know, that I should call out the Black Shirts, many of whom are chewing the bit and growing impatient." *Mussolini,* speech at Cremona.

June 19. "There are certain Italian political corpses, who delude themselves with the idea that they are still living because they are abusing our generosity. We shall no longer do them the honour of regarding them as enemies. . . . Black Shirts of Tuscany and Florence, if it is necessary to re-commence, will you re-commence?" *Mussolini,* speech at Florence.

June 25. "The Fascists are entering some dwellings in order to remind recalcitrants of their duty to vote." *L'Intrepido,* a Fascist daily paper in Lucca.

July 8. "The Fascist revolution made the mistake of not bringing before a special tribunal of National Defence the wretched Senator who is betraying the Dalmatians by an infamous campaign. But many Fascists have not forgotten, and will not forget to the end of their lives, Albertini's [2] betrayal." *Popolo d'Italia.*

July 8. "The subversives have found unhoped-for allies in the Liberalism of Luigi Albertini and the Popularism of Luigi Sturzo,[3] and in the interminable disputes of Fascism in these latter days. . . . To these two must be added the name of Filippo Turati. The conviction that the Fascist Government is now impregnable, also feeds the exasperation of the brutalised followers of the Red creed. While the Government is on the watch and is ordering the arrest of subversives and the raking in of arms on a vast scale, the possibility still remains that the series of treacherous crimes may con-

[2] Senator Albertini is the editor of the *Corriere della Sera,* the great Liberal daily.—*Trans.*
[3] Don Luigi Sturzo was the founder and leader until recently of the Catholic Popular Party.—*Trans.*

tinue, despite the application of measures of exceptional and unmitigated rigour." *Volta newsagency,* official announcement.

July 8. "For some days there has been a recurrence of Socialist crimes. Very well! We say candidly that the responsibility for this bloodshed falls on those Liberal leaders who, with their stupid polemics, are putting mistaken ideas into the heads of the lower strata of society as to the possibility of Socialist recovery. . . . Fascism will go inexorably to work, and will reply pitilessly to the shedding of Fascist blood for which the Red band of hooligans is making itself responsible. The responsibility for the disorder falls exclusively on the heads of certain Liberals. We level against them this public accusation and warning. Let them beware of abusing Fascist patience!" *Popolo d'Italia.* (Mussolini's paper.)

July. "Should the anticipated opposition of the Chamber to the draft electoral reform measure show itself in an adverse vote upsetting the bill, the Prime Minister would remain tranquilly at his place in the battlefield, which he has occupied for six months with the fervid consent of the Nation, and would not deviate from his inexorable path; he has held in his hand since the glorious days of October the decree closing the Chamber." *Official communication to the press.*

July 13. "If the Acerbo bill is rejected, defeatist parliamentarism will be marching to its doom. . . . This is the only conclusion, and there is only one path for Fascism: be prepared! . . .

"We are now in this situation because in October, 1922, through excessive good faith, we did not carry through completely a revolution which should have been inexorable. Mischievous men such as Nitti, Treves, Turati, Modigliani, Serrati and Albertini should be committed to a tribunal of National Defence. Poison-

ous vipers are not coddled and allowed their freedom."
Popolo d'Italia.

July 25. "So long as the State has not become completely Fascist, so long, that is, as there has not been completely carried out, in all the State administrations and institutions, the replacement of the directing class of yesterday by a directing class of Fascists or of members of sworn allegiance to Fascism, . . . the Government, which made the revolution and has assumed all the responsibilities it involves, will be unable to dispense with the armed force of the Black Shirts."
Mussolini, declaration to the Fascist Grand Council.

July 31. "Brought up to 500,000, the Black Shirts constitute the formidable army destined to guarantee the continuity of the Fascist Government. . . The mischievous and underhand Sicilian priest [1] and his party following must be considered as enemies of the Government and of Fascism; the same applies to the Unitary Socialists who have grouped themselves around the old and worn-out lay figures of Reformism." *Grand Fascist Council.*

* * * * *

September 1. Against the local clergy: "We shall exhume an *ardito's*[2] blade from the trenches where we learned the quick stab which rips a man open like a pig." *Il Fascista,* an Alba paper.

October 11. "When the pig of Basilicata[3] was in power he allowed the civil servants to celebrate the first of May. . . . Revolutions have their rights and it is not well to leave them unfulfilled. . . . In spite of Cagoia, there will be formidable celebrations of the march on Rome, and the ten thousand banners which will defile through the capital will impress vividly upon

[1] Don Sturzo.
[2] The *arditi* were the Italian shock troops.—*Trans.*
[3] Signor Nitti.—*Trans.*

79

all the rabble that Italy is still in arms not only against the pestilential subversives, but also against Cagoia and his skinny, miserable clerics. . ." *Popolo d'Italia.* (Mussolini's paper.)

October 22. "If the (internal) enemies move, we must have the courage to post guards with fixed bayonets, to say: 'Halt! No thoroughfare!'" *Giunta,* speech to the Fascist Trade Unions.

October 24. " . . . Three days after the Naples congress we took Rome, and began the work of scraping and cleaning which is not yet finished and must continue." *Mussolini,* speech at Turin.

October 28. " . . . I beg you, Fascists, to bear in mind that the revolution was the work of cudgels. What have you in your hands now?" (The Fascists shout: "Rifles, bombs, machine-guns!") "If to-morrow the alarm were sounded, the signal for those great days which decide the destiny of peoples, would you respond?" ("Yes, we swear it!") " . . . If to-morrow I told you that you must continue the march to the end, but in other directions, would you march?" ("Yes.") " . . . The Fascist Government will last because we shall systematically scatter our enemies. . . ." *Mussolini,* speech at Milan.

November 7. "The repeated and foolish attempts of the many-coloured opposition parties, ranging from Luigi Albertini to Enrico Malatesta, excite no apprehension. . . . Similar attempts were made at Milan by the Unitary Socialists, who tried to engineer a base political trick, taking advantage of the turning back of a procession to celebrate victory—a speculation honestly and rightfully suppressed by the Fascists. . . . . There is an opinion that all this is the prelude to the formation of a single libero-demo-social-anarchico-republico-popular-Sturzian front. Such a single front has already been once thrown into utter confusion, in

August, 1922. . . . To-day the task of burying, once for all, the opposition parties *en bloc* is much easier. The Black Shirts only await a word of command." *Volta Agency,* official communication.

November 26. "For some time past, Count Sforza [1] —marquis of falsehood—has been active in political and diplomatic circles, trying to bury in oblivion the shamelessness which has for ever exiled him from Italian diplomacy and political life. That Count Sforza should still show activity, now that he has escaped from the castor oil which the Fascists of his country intended justly to administer to him, is comprehensible, but it is not so easy to understand the line of conduct adopted by M. Barrère,[2] who ought to be beginning to realise that in Fascist Italy greater discretion is absolutely necessary. . . ." *Popolo d'Italia.*

November 29. "Four hundred officers of militia, ready to kill and to die for their country and for Fascism, send to the *'Duce'* ('leader') of the new Italy their most faithful and formidable *A noi*! ('Up and at them!') *Signed*: De Bono, Fara, Sacco, Belloni, Gagliano, Terruzzi, Agostini, Guglielmotti, Vermè, Ragioni." *Telegram to Signor Mussolini from Naples,* sent by De Bono, director-general of the National Militia.

November 23. "Around the *Duce* there is a tumult of joyfully-beating hearts and an unbreakable barrier of arms and armed men. The former is the proof of consent; the latter will show force when necessary, and will make it prevail." *Popolo d'Italia.*

"Although Fascism is a typically Italian phenomenon, there is no doubt that some of its postulates are of a universal order, since many countries have suffered and are suffering from the degeneration of democratic and

[1] Formerly Foreign Minister. He was Ambassador in Paris in 1922, and resigned that post on Signor Mussolini's accession to power.—*Trans.*
[2] French ambassador in Rome.—*Trans.*

liberal systems" *Mussolini,* to Primo De Rivera, during a banquet at the Palazzo Venezia.

November 24. "Nitti is something worse than a thing of no acount; he cannot show himself in public without being spat at; he is a man in the position of those offenders whom a justice more primitive, but certainly more exemplary, would mark with the brand of infamy.

This cannot go on, and the time has come for deeds instead of words, to show the gangrenous remains of this discarded old ruin that the Fascist generosity which spared him the firing squad demands in return at least silence. . ." *Idea Nazionale.* (Rome Nationalist paper.)

November 30. "Yesterday evening, about 7 o'clock, some 500 Fascists of proved boldness . . gathered before Signor Nitti's house and commenced a formidable chorus of imprecations. Some hundreds of more exasperated Fascists began to fire at the walls of the house, and two strong groups attacked the railings. Some policemen who came running up were knocked over, and one of them went away to give the alarm at the Police Station. Meanwhile the Fascists had broken into the premises, and, still firing, smashed the ground floor shutters with clubs.

"The group which got inside hunted for Nitti, but without success. . . .

"The political secretary of the Roman Fascio has warned us against the enemies within the country, to whom the Fascist revolution left full liberty to plot, and has added that the capital cannot tolerate Nitti's insulting attitude. If the plots continue, if no precautions are taken against the defeatist Press, Fascism will inevitably break the vicious circle and resume its interrupted march. . . .

"Owing to the conscienceless and intolerable campaign of certain Nittian newspapers, Fascism has this evening broken the bonds which it has imposed upon itself since the march on Rome, and has returned to the good old legendary days of action.   The crafty Opposition has received a warning, and Fascism throughout Italy will learn to-morrow that there are perhaps at hand fresh days of strife, for which everyone is already prepared and resolved." *Corriere Italiano.* (Fascist paper of Rome.)

PART IV.

—AND THE CHRONICLE OF DEEDS.[1]

MAY, 1923.

Genoa.—At Marassi-Guezzi Fascists strike workmen found in public bars, fire revolver and rifle shots, and set fire to the Friendly Society's premises.

Leonessa.—Fascists command the Marshal of Carabineers to arrest four workers who had sung the "Red Flag."

Rome.—The placarding of manifestoes and of announcements of meetings is prohibited. Workers ordered to resume work on pain of dismissal.

Rome.—Workers distributing leaflets for May-day arrested. The Fascist Militia tear the red carnations from passers-by.

Domodossola.—Fascists wait for Socialists coming out of a meeting and assault them, wounding two.

Arzignano (Vicenza).—The manufacturer Pelizzari ordered by Fascists to dismiss immediately twelve workers who had celebrated May-day.

Genoa.—A carabineer, Berretta Amedeo, beaten by Fascists, and obliged to undergo hospital treatment.

Jesi.—The local silk works ordered to close down because the workwomen had celebrated May-day.

Milan.—Chamber of Labour entered during the night, and an attempt made to set it on fire.

Cavenago Brianza.—A local club attacked, furniture and banners being burned.

Zelo Surigone (Brianza). — Portalupi Vittorio, together with his father, beaten in his own house by Fascists.

---

[1] The Report gives the chronicle of thirteen months' atrocities. The record of two typical months, May and November of last year (1923), is given in the following pages.—*Trans.*

Sesto S. Giovanni.—A workman named Carlo Vignati beaten by Fascists, and taken to hospital with grave signs of concussion.

Naples.—The Chamber of Labour laid waste.

Milan.—The worker Galdi Gerolamo wounded whilst at a club, and obliged to go to hospital.

Parma.—The worker Tosini Guido killed by Fascists.

Parma.—The Deputy Picelli insulted and threatened; the worker Maluberti Enrico, a war hero, decorated with one bronze and two silver medals, beaten; Campanini Pietro, a war invalid, seriously wounded.

Brescia.—The Fascist Militia thrash the workers holidaying in suburban inns.

Florence.—The police search for, seize and remove manifestoes.

Venice.—The police arrest the secretary of a co-operative society and thrash any workers who celebrated May-day. Fascists, thinking that they were firing on "subversives" celebrating May-day, kill Piciaccia and another worker named Gusti.

Milan.—Fascists attack a restaurant in the Strada Paullese, where dancing is going on, and fire a revolver at the mechanic Gerolamo Galdi, wounding him.

Rome.—Fascists make their way into a café and wound De Silveri, and then seriously wound the employee Giovanni Rotoli by stabbing him in the chest.

Quezzi (Genoa).—Fascists attack a Friendly Society, and set fire to it on account of a hymn written to be sung on May-day. Damage, 100,000 lire.

Naples.—Workers returning to work after celebrating May-day, met with cudgels and revolvers. Three seriously wounded: Pasquale Musella, Giuseppe Riccardi, Gennaro Benincasa.

Carrara.—Fascists occupy the premises of the

Republican party, and order the closing of establishments deserted on May-day.

Bitonto.—Antonio Bonassia, member of the Catholic League, killed by Fascist militiamen, and another worker seriously wounded.

Cavenago Brianza.—Twenty Fascists arrive in a lorry, attack the club, beat the workers, set the place on fire and make off firing revolver shots. Damage, 15,000 lire.

Lumezzano (Brescia).—Fascists beat a septuagenarian because he had stayed away from work on May-day.

Stellata (Ferrara).—For having celebrated May-day, Enzo Zaniratti, a war cripple, assaulted and brutally beaten at night.

Mantua.—The provincial Fascist Secretariat proposes the dismissal of workers who celebrated May-day.

Rome.—The police give notice to contractors to dismiss many bricklayers who had taken part in the May-day celebrations; more than a hundred arrested and obliged to return to the villages whence they had been banished by the violence of the Fascists.

A Fascist leader demands that the Prefect should take rigorous steps against a group of workers who were absent from work on May-day.

Florence.—The mechanic Bencini Antonio beaten by Fascists for absence from work on May-day.

Poggio a Caiano.—The merchants, Allori Bros., beaten by five Fascists.

Varese.—Fascists beat Domenico Camillucci di Orino and drive him from his district.

Galeata (Florence).—Fascists assault and beat those present at a funeral party which several Socialists are attending.

Bozzolo (Mantua).—The engineer Giovanni Vialli, decorated with the silver medal for war service, is severely beaten by three Fascists and banished from the Commune where he works.

Bisceglie.—As a reprisal the Fascists set fire to the premises of the Republican section and of the Bricklayers' League.

Cusano Milanino.—Fifteen Fascists attack the Socialist Co-operative Society, and wound Antonio Rusconi.

Uggiate (Como).—The parish priest Salvatore Sironi banished from the district.

Biella.—The Socialist Giardini Selvini, secretary of the Textile League, assaulted and beaten by Fascists.

Pompeii.—Several Fascists illtreat some young ladies who were carrying red flowers to the Madonna.

S. Prospero Strinati.—Morini Raimondo, manager of the Consumers' Co-operative Society, beaten by Fascists.

Ferentino (Rome).—Catholic youths assaulted and beaten for wearing the badges of their associations.

Bitonto.—The Socialist Buonavia Gaetano shot with a revolver by Fascists and killed. In the same mélée the worker Francesco Giorgi seriously wounded.

Alessandria.—Conflict between Fascist railway police and other Fascists. Alessandria station invaded and numerous rifle shots fired ; several wounded.

Viareggio.—Attack on the Republican Hall.

Pistoia.—The Masonic Lodge in Corso Vittorio Emanuele attacked by Fascists, who carry away administrative material and objects.

Borgosesia.—The manufacturers Dominietto and Chiarino beaten.

Bologna.—The worker Buldrini Primo taken to hospital, having been beaten by Fascists.

Brescia.—Groups of Fascists, armed with sticks, post themselves at the exit of the Zust establishment and beat many of the workers.

Brescia.—The Socialist Martinini beaten till the blood came, on his way out of a building. Fascists set fire to the library of the Universal Friendly Society.

Belluno.—The ex-deputy Santin obliged to leave the town immediately by order of the Fascists.

Ravenna.—Fascists prevent the christening of children in the church, threatening interference.

Pesaro.—Doctor Sandro Fabris, secretary of the Labour Union, beaten by Fascists.

Bognanco (Novara).—The Socialist clubs laid waste.

Naples.—Conflict between Fascists and ex-service railwaymen.

Rumianca (Novara).—The Socialist clubs of Rumianca, Vogogna, Piedimulera destroyed by Fascists as a reprisal.

Brescia.—The tramwayman Ghitti Giuseppe beaten by Fascists.

Gardone Val Trompia.—Cinelli, secretary of the "Fiom" (Bricklayers' Union), banished from his district by Fascists.

Gurone (Varese). The Socialist Pagani Tranquilo surprised in his own house by Fascists, carried outside, beaten and stabbed. His wife, screaming with fear, is threatened with revolvers.

Odolo (Brescia).—Fascists lay waste the local workers' club and offices.

Canicatti.—Two Communists attacked and wounded for wearing a red poppy in their buttonhole.

Pontremoli.—The local Council of the Popular Party resigns on account of continual Fascist violence.

Pesaro.—Doctor Andrea Fabbri, secretary of the Unione Popolare (Popular Party Association), beaten by Fascists.

Bologna.—In the hall of the assize court the lawyer Guerrisi Giuseppe is insulted and threatened for defending Socialists.

Chieti.—The Socialist lawyer Magno Galliano beaten by Fascists.

Grumello (Bergamo).—The propagandist Zanga, of the Popular Party, attacked by Fascists in his own office, accompanied to the station, and forced to quit the district immediately.

Leonessa.—Members of the local Fascist directory insult and threaten the administrative body, prevent it from continuing its work, and order the dissolution of the Communal Council.

Palma Montechiaro.—A Fascist strikes a ten-year-old child who is singing the "Red Flag." Mazza Rosalia, the mother of the child, reduced to a sad plight, being bitten and thrashed.

Udine.—Monsignor Isolo forbidden to take part in a procession at Gemona.

Ancona.—A steamer arrived from Russia laden with grain. Fascists prevent the sailors from landing.

Prato.—The entrance of the Masonic Lodge forced. Furniture, books, insignia, and utensils destroyed.

Bosco Marengo (Alessandria). — Fascists throw bombs at a group of persons, wounding several. At the same time the worker Zuccotti killed by a revolver shot.

Naples.—Fascists lay waste the Naples Chamber of Labour a second time, beating the organisers found inside.

Ravenna.—Fascists occupy the Republican club quarters.

Sale di Gussago (Brescia).—The *Popolari*[1] Paderini, Lazzaroni, and Angioli, beaten by Fascists; they will take a fortnight to recover.

Bologna.—The house of the farmer Gaetano Piretti attacked, and he and his son Luigi compelled to follow the assailants to the offices of the Fascio. They obey, but on reaching the open country are shot. The son killed, and the father seriously wounded.

Catania.—Bands of Fascists chase and beat several townspeople because they wear in the buttonholes of their jackets badges which do not find favour with the Fascists.

Francavilla.—Prof. Concetto Parisi, of the Popular Party, assaulted and struck while entering his house. The deputy Lombardo-Pellegrino arrested in his own house.

Naples.—Fascists fire revolver shots at the Chamber of Labour.

Pistoia.—Fascist militiamen arrest Count Carlo Matteucci, propagandist of the D'Annunzian "Fascio Spirituale."

Penne.—The Republican De Caesaris beaten; he had only come out of hospital a few days before, after an attempt at suicide.

Reggio.—Bellentani Leopoldo and Bellelli Bruno beaten by Fascists.

Casola Canossa (R. Emilia).—Don Serafino Vessani threatened and struck by Fascists.

Rovigo.—The Socialist Zangrossi Arturo exiled by the Fascists.

Uggiate (Como).—Don Sironi, parish priest, seized by Fascists, carried round the streets, and exposed to the derision of passers-by.

Parma.—A score of excursionists assaulted by a large

[1] Members of the Catholic Popular Party.—*Trans.*

number of Fascists. They declare that they belong to no party, but are beaten all the same.

Cantù.—A band of Fascists proceed to Montorfano, madly firing revolvers, and beat and injure Luigi Agliati, a war cripple.

Nubolera (Brescia).—Signor Ballerini, head of the Catholic League, assaulted and struck by Fascists.

The house of the woman teacher Lambia Maria attacked.

Lucera.—Fascists beat wearers of red carnations and red handkerchiefs.

Rome.—Dissident Fascists attempt to occupy the Palazzo Marignoli. Collisions and wounding among the Fascists.

Palermo.—Fascists with revolvers threaten and hold up bricklayers wearing the "Soldino" badge.

Brescia.—Fascists lay waste the clubs of Inzano and Baldeniga.

Novara.—The premises of the Francesco Ferrer Club entered, banners and administrative material taken away, and the councillors present ruthlessly beaten.

Avigliano (Turin).—Groups of Fascists burst into the Council Hall of the Commune, and demand the resignation of the councillors.

Bologna.—The worker Zucchini Otello, whilst entering his house, is assaulted and struck by a disorderly crowd of Fascists. At the hospital it is expected that he will take twenty days to recover.

Cesano Maderno.—Incidents between *Popolari* and the Fascists in a religious procession. A rifle shot from the offices of the Fascio kills Narciso Mangani. A Fascist expedition on lorries attacks the houses and premises of Catholics during the night, arresting and wounding the occupiers. Among the more seriously wounded are Lorenzo Elli, Angelo Grossi, and Luigi Grossi, all members of the Popular Party. Instead of punishing the guilty parties, the parish priest, Don Arrigoni, and another priest are arrested.

Musocco (Milan).—Fascists arrive in motor cars, enter the Socialist club, and beat two workers.

Avellino.—Fascists go on a punitive expedition, setting a house on fire, holding up a religious festival, and firing through the streets. They destroy the railways workers' club, beating workers and Socialists.

Palermo.—Fascists fire revolver shots at the demonstrators wearing the "Soldino" badge.[1] The coachman Gerlando di Natale seriously wounded.

Naples.—Collisions and incidents between Fascists and Dissident Fascists; some wounded and some arrested.

Secondigliano (Naples).—The club quarters of the Young Catholic Scouts destroyed.

Gardone Val Trompia.—The house of Bosio in the hamlet of Onzino entered; the Fascists fire with sporting rifles at the unfortunate man, striking him full in the chest, and leaving him in a desperate condition.

Varese.—The Fascio puts a veto on the inauguration ceremony of an art school because the members of the Chamber of Labour are invited.

Genoa.—The premises of the "Alba Proletaria" friendly society set on fire by Fascists. The damage is estimated at 200,000 lire.

---

[1] King Victor Emanuel visited Naples in this month, and his visit was made the occasion of great monarchist demonstrations, of a decidedly anti-Fascist character, all over Southern Italy. (The hold of Fascism in the South has throughout been weak.) A press communique was issued warning all who "use loyalty as a mask" for anti-Fascist demonstrations! The demonstrators wore a *soldo* (halfpenny), with the King's effigy on it, in their button-holes.—*Trans.*

Naples.—In a conflict provoked by Fascists the young woman Giovanna Virgilio is killed.

Lecco.—Two Fascists brandish revolvers, and one kills the other, a youth of 19 years

Mesagne (Brindisi).—Conflicts with Fascists. Several Socialist workers wounded.

Rome.—On leaving Parliament after a speech in the Chamber against certain proceedings of the Fascist Government, the Deputy Alfredo Misuri is assaulted and beaten, and has to be taken in all haste to the hospital, where he must remain for some weeks. The band of bullies was brought expressly from Bologna.

Trivero (Novara).—The Co-operative broken into and laid waste.

Asti.—In the house of the Deputy Vigna a group of Socialists are gathered together to meet Emilio Zannerini, a member of the Executive of the party. The police break into the hall and proceed to make a search. One by one, as those taking part in the meeting go out, they are beaten by Fascists.

Leghorn.—Nine Communists and the Deputy Belloni arrested, on account of a plot later recognised as non-existent.

Borgoratti (Genoa).—Fifteen Fascists lay waste the "Felice Cavalotti" friendly society.

Genoa.—During the night a group of Fascists attack the tramwaymen Isaia Rossi, Alberghi Stefano, Gandini Alessandro. The latter are obliged to go to hospital for medical treatment.

Rome.—The Fascists assault an amateur dramatic society of the Popular Party, illtreating those present, both ladies and gentlemen.

Chiaravalle.—The quarters of the Republican group attacked, and everything found there burned. The

Fascists also try to remove from the entrance to the hall the memorial tablet which records the names of the 28 Republicans who fell in the war.

Chieti.—The coachman Alfredo Pucci beaten, and the carabineers ordered to arrest him for having whistled the "Red Flag."

Turin.—Pietro Gobetti, a Liberal journalist, searched and arrested.

Ramatto (Catania).—The Fascists order the local military band to go and receive Commendatore Starace. On these ex-service men refusing, the Fascists proceed to violence, wounding several persons.

Solzago (Como).—A band of Fascists proceeds to Tavernetto under the pretext of making a search, and throws the entire quarter into uproar.

Bologna.—The workers Malossi Enea, Artizzani Amedeo and Zanoni Giovanni beaten by Fascists. Their contused wounds will take a fortnight to heal.

Cogna (Arezzo).—A dozen Fascists enter the house of the Monetti family, beating all the members of the family, and shooting dead Monetti Settimio because he attempted to escape.

Palma Montechiaro.—A group of Fascists throw a kinema hall into disorder, provoking a panic, in which Scopeliti is seriously injured.

Minerva (Verona).—The population, through a committee, protests in the daily newspapers against the intimidation practised by the Fascists during the elections for the Council.

Rovato.—The Syndic refuses to receive in the town hall certain Fascist leaders, and on that account is beaten.

Novara.—The engine driver Ruschi Raffaello struck and insulted by Fascists.

Viverone (Novara).—Fascists disturb and break up a meeting of Liberals. Amongst those beaten are Prof. Emanuele Sella, and the accountant Dante Coda, who has the silver medal for war service.

Parma.—Carpi Gino, a volunteer during the war, assaulted in the night by Fascists, and wounded with a cudgel.

Sampierdarena. — Fascists order the Socialist Barbareschi to suspend a subscription amongst the workers on behalf of four comrades killed on duty. They prevent the members of the Chamber of Labour from attending the funeral, and beat Barbareschi.

Rolo.—Righi Telemaco and Lodi Antonio beaten by Fascists.

NOVEMBER, 1923.

Musocco (Milan).—Fascists invade a Popular Party Club, cut out two medallions there, damage the furniture and daub varnish over everything.

Rome.—About a hundred Sardinian Fascists meet a certain Peddussa Luigi of Nuovo, and beat him because he carries in his buttonhole the badge of the Sardinian Party.

Lazzale (Milan).—Fascists invade the Co-operative Stores, smash the furniture, destroy the stock of foodstuffs, drive out those present and chase them through the streets.

Parelo (Genoa).—Fascists proceed to the house of the President of the ex-Servicemen's Association, make him get out of bed, and beat him. They also beat various other ex-servicemen.

Biella.—On the arrival of the train, all the copies of the Turin *Stampa* are taken to the Piazza Cavour and destroyed.

Bologna.—A workman named Benfanati Ercole beaten with cudgels.

Incisa Valdarno.—Two Fascists make an armed attack on a Fascist named Luigi Falorni, because he and his family prevented the aggressors from driving a motor car at full speed.

Belfiore (Foligno).—Fascists, armed and masked, threaten with revolvers and wound workmen named Casciola Paolo and Amedeo Vanga. The Deputy Innamorati threatened by Fascists with knives and ordered to leave the district at once.

Rome.—Fascists go to the office of the *Popolo,* threaten those present, and cut the wires of the telephone instruments. A young Catholic named Callucci, who protests, is punched and kicked. The office doorkeeper also struck.

Gualdo Tadino (Umbria).—A band of Fascists, armed and masked, attack with cudgels several citizens, including a Socialist named Pannunzio, who is left on the ground senseless and bleeding.

Milan.—Fascists forcibly prevent the Unitary Socialists from taking part in the procession organised by the Association of the Wounded, on the anniversary of the Armistice. After the usual insults and threats, the Fascists attack groups of Socialists who are taking their places in the procession. The Deputy Gonzales receives a heavy blow on the side from a cudgel, and his wife, interposing to defend him, only just succeeds in avoiding a blow aimed at her with a club by a Fascist. Among those injured are Vigorelli and Valente, who were wounded in the war and decorated for bravery, and others. After resisting the attacks, the Socialists separated to the cry of "Long live free Italy !"

Oneglia.—The ex-councillors of the former Socialist Commune are taking part in a patriotic procession, when the Fascists rush at them and strike them with cudgels. The injured include the ex-Syndic Piana.

Biella. The Deputy Savio is in company with the Senator Marco Pozzo and other lawyers, discussing local problems, when insulting gestures are made at him by men of the National Militia. Savio takes no notice, but nevertheless is kicked, punched, and slapped in the face.

Catania.—Offices of the Provincial Council occupied.

Nicolisi and Centuripe (Catania).—On the occasion of the Council elections armed Fascists block the streets.

Brindisi.—The provincial Fascist trade union proceeds to occupy the Custom House.

Pietrasanta.—Four cars full of Fascists from Massa, armed with rifles and revolvers, arrive in the night. One group of them stand on guard outside the carabineers' barracks; another breaks up the sign which reads "Lucca Gate" and substitutes "Massa Gate."

Mantua.—Eleven arrests made at Asola, 21 at Mosio on the Chiese, and the houses of many "subversives" searched.

Florence.—In consequence of the Amnesty Decree, various Socialists are released from prison, but all at once fall victims to Fascist outrages. At Bagno a Ripoli, the Fascists cudgel the released prisoners Giannini and Pratesi; and at Scandisei,Michelassi.

Monsummano.—At 10 o'clock at night four Fascists attack and wound a workman named Livi.

Pomigliano.—The tomb of Matteo Renato Imbriani outraged. The widow protests vigorously, and lodges an accusation against the Fascists responsible.

Cesena.—Fascists cudgel Dr. Mario Bistocchi, editor of *Italia del Popolo.*

Foiano della Chiana.—After being kept out of the district for two years, Rampi Alfredo, formerly chairman of the local Socialist League, returns home to arrange some private affairs. A gang of 15 Fascists meet him near his house, insult him, and beat him until the blood runs.

Pavia.—Prof. Malagugini, ex-Syndic of Pavia, savagely beaten by Fascists because he is believed to be the author of a communication published by the Socialist daily, *Giustizia.* The same treatment is meted out to Dr. Cantoni.

Pesaro.—Fascists cudgel the magistrate Signor Ebner, because he did not lift his hat when one of their banners passed.

Avezzano.—Socialists named De Jullis, Orsini, and De Sanctis attacked and savagely beaten.

Fossola (Carrara).—Fascists murder a Republican named Calmanti Giovanni, and gravely wound his brother Pietro with revolver shots.

Novate Milanese.—The local club invaded; those present beaten with cudgels.

Turro.—Fascists enter a restaurant and force those present to proceed to the Fascist headquarters, where they are beaten with cudgels.

Tortona.—Fascists attack, strike, and wound in the head the lawyer Alessandro Barenghi, correspondent of the *Corriere della Sera.*

Milan.—A band of arditi attacked by a band of Fascists because they are wearing the black shirt. One of the former, named Biasi, while in bed, is invited to the Fascist headquarters (named after Cesare Battisti), and, on arrival, is cudgelled and wounded.

Tortona.—A dissident Fascist named Giovanni Angeleri seriously wounds in the eye a Fascist named Rossi Ettore. In return, the Fascists hunt for Angeleri, and when they find him, beat him till the blood runs.

Asti.—Fascists attack and seriously wound the Deputy Scotti for conducting propaganda in favour of the organisation of the farm-labourers.

Naples.—Fascists of Barra, assembled near their headquarters, savagely strike and wound a Communist named Perma Raffaele, whom they accuse of—a provocative attitude !

Bergamo.—At Sarnico, Fascists attack and savagely strike, without any reason, a group of workmen who are quietly walking home.

Novara.—Fascists, on the pretence of requiring medical attention for a wounded man, get into the house of Dr. Cavaliere Domenico Grandi, and beat him till the blood runs, in the presence of his family, for having said that a workman, wounded by the Fascists, would not be well for a fortnight, instead of a week.

Bagnacavallo (Ravenna).—A Fascist militiaman named Bruno dall' Oglio shot four times with a revolver, and killed, by a Fascist named Montanari Giovanni.

Trino.—The provincial Fascist Delegate orders the Syndic to resign because he is not a Fascist. On his refusing, he is threatened with a concentration of Black Shirts, and "reprisals."

Camisano Vicentino.—The Popular Party Communal administration driven out with violence by a band of Black Shirts.

Arezzo.—Fascists arrive and invade a room where a workmen's committee is seated, and proceed to hit out with cudgels and fire revolvers. A workman named Gavilli Amedeo severely wounded in the abdomen, and when taken to hospital has to have a serious operation.

Varese.—At Locate Varesino, Fascists present themselves at the ex-servicemen's Co-operative, because the latter have used the phrase "Sun of the future" in the ticket of invitation to a festival. They attack with cudgels and revolvers. One of the ex-servicemen, a workman named Ramponi Guglielmo, is killed.

Asti.—Many incidents and cudgel fights between official and dissident Fascists. The latter accuse the Deputy Torre of having ordered the transfer from Turin to Reggio Calabria of a dissident Fascist named Gentile, an accountant.

Venice.—Fascists break into the S. Antonio Club and wreck it.

Monsummano.—A peasant named Bartoletti attacked and beaten by four Fascists till the blood comes. A few months previously this man was forced to swallow castor oil and to allow his face to be smeared with soot, and was then exposed to the derision of the Fascists and compelled to make a declaration.

Florence.—A Socialist railwayman named Rimbotti beaten by the Fascists till the blood runs, because he is supposed to have spoken slightingly of them. He is later threatened with violence because a "subversive" newspaper gives a short account of what had previously happened to him.

Pizzidimonte (Prato).—Six Fascist militiamen shoot in the night at Nuti Adamo and kill him.

Zenon di Piave.—A band of Fascist militiamen on their way back from Treviso compel the public bars to close, and cudgel a man named Caurazian, disabled in the war.

Mezzo Lombardo (Trento).—A numerous band of Fascists drive the Syndic to the Town Hall, where he is exposed to a hostile demonstration. Later on the Fascists occupy the Council Chamber, and finally order the members to hand in their resignations by the 27th of the month.

At the Golden Cross inn certain Fascists threaten

and insult the Syndic, and draw revolvers with the object of intimidating him.

In consequence of the threats and pressure from the Fascists the Communal Council resigns, declaring that it is no longer in a position to carry out its duties freely.

Florence.—In the S. Salvi quarter, in a public bar, the wife of a discharged railwayman utters bitter words about the authors of the measure under which her husband has suffered. A few hours later the woman is insulted by local Fascists, dragged to the police barracks and kept in the guardroom all night.

Livorno Piemonte.—A Socialist named Bellotto Eugenio is attacked by the Fascists, and is beaten with cudgels on his way to the polling-booth.

Naples.—Fascists and *arditi,* contending for precedence in a procession in honour of the King of Spain, jostle one another, with their hands on their daggers.

On the same day a band of Fascists fire off revolvers, causing a panic among the dock labourers and boatmen. On the following morning Leandro Brussar, a Dutch sailor, is found dead with a bullet wound in the throat, and later on the corpses of another sailor and a boatman are found.

Near the "Trianon" the Fascists fire hundreds of revolver shots, and order the citizens to shut their windows. On this occasion, a passer-by named Antonio Anguilli is bayonetted in the back.

Mirandola.—A band of Fascist militiamen, with a regular warrant, summon to the barracks, at about midnight, a certain Beraldi, and demand that he should make a declaration that he has violated his own daughter, made her a mother, and hidden the child. The accused firmly denies the charge, and so rouses the wrath of his self-constituted judges, who belabour him with cudgels. The unfortunate man's cries were heard —but without result—from the barracks, which is actually in the building of the sub-prefecture. Beraldi is carried out dead, and from a subsequent examination of the numerous contusions on various parts of the body, and especially on the head, it is proved that death was due to the blows dealt against him.

Carrara.—As a reprisal for homicide, the Fascists give chase to the brothers Secchiari, one of whom is killed by a rifle shot, while the other falls down a precipitous ravine and is seriously injured.

Brescia.—A group of Fascist militiamen attack a peasant family, striking them with the butts of their rifles. Andrea Gnocchi, 70 years of age, so seriously wounded that he dies shortly afterwards.

Rome.—A large band of Fascists set off from the centre of the city for the house of Signor Nitti, ex-Prime Minister, on the other side of the Tiber. A great number of revolver and rifle shots fired both inside and outside the house. The furniture destroyed, the members of the household threatened, etc. The police arrive when it is all over.

———

The foregoing is only a list of some typical instances of the manifestations of Fascist lawlessness which were continuous in the first year of Fascist government. Lawlessness is now a permanent feature, especially in some parts of Italy, where the law and the constitution and the very organs of the law have been superseded, lawless government being imposed on the citizens by violence or, in the end, merely by threats of violence.

The things that have been possible, especially in the rural communes, with the open connivance of the governing authorities, in cases where the citizens have shown any sign of a perfectly legitimate resistance, are exemplified in the history of Molinella, a small commune of less than 15,000 inhabitants in the Province of Bologna.

PART V.

THE CONQUEST OF MOLINELLA.

September, 1922. General boycott. In the month of September the Fascio and the big farmers ordered a boycott of the workers who were members of the Labour Co-operatives of Molinella. It should be mentioned that the great majority of the employers were bound by working contracts still in force (many had been in force for several years), each one signed at the employment bureau of these Co-operatives. The contracts were thus broken, and from that day no one was permitted to take on workers. Even in the government drainage works at Reno, although no boycott had been declared, work was constantly being interrupted, and there was continual obstructionism, with long suspensions of work which came just at the moments when the farmers' offensive against the organised workers was as its most violent phase. While the boycott was thus declared (it still continues) and applied to local workers, and while during the summer of 1923 thousands of men and women were thus totally unemployed, workers from Ferrara, Venetia and the districts bordering the Bolognese were being imported into the Commune, notwithstanding that they cost much more and did less work than the local workers.

September 12. The Fascists set fire to the headquarters of the workers' and peasants' organisations, in which were the offices of the Communal Committee, and the Communal Employment Bureaux for labourers, bricklayers, and metal workers. Everything was destroyed, including the large building. The offices were then transferred to the premises of the Agricultural Co-operative Society, and its Agricultural Machine Depôt, in the Via Malborghetto.

October 29. The new premises of the workers' organisations and the Communal Committee, as well as the premises of the Agricultural Co-operative Society, the Agricultural Machine Depôt, the People's Library and the kilns, were attacked by Fascists. They took everything away, tables, chairs, typewriters, and anything else they found. Afterwards no one was permitted to enter, and on November 20 the Fascists themselves installed a new tenant, who is still there.

October 29. The district Employment Bureau of Marmorta, part of the Commune, was attacked by Fascists, who burned papers and registers, remained there until November 5, and then locked up the place —and woe to whoever approached it! In the last fortnight of December the secretary of the Fascio came with a lorry, loaded up everything—tables, cupboards, etc.—and took them no one knows where. In April, 1923, the Fascist trade union took up its quarters there, and it is there to this day.

October 29. The district Employment Bureau of S. Pietro Capofiume, part of the Commune, was also attacked by Fascists, who carried off everything, and installed there as tenant the Fascist farmer Carlotti Giuseppe.

October 29. The Employment Bureau of S. Martino in Argine was attacked by Fascists, who handed the place over to the landlord who had let it, enjoining him never again to let the workers' organisations have it.

October 30. A band of armed Fascists entered and occupied the quarters of the Employment Bureau of Selva, part of Molinella, and the Co-operative wine shop attached to it. The Fascists, after having taken the keys by force, handed them to the landlord, Selleri Pietro. Since that date everything has been carried away, and the keys of the place are still in the hands of the above-named Fascist landlord.

October 31. The secretary of the Communal Committee, Fabbri Paolo, and three members, Bentivoglio Giuseppe, Toschi Marcello and Schiassi Carlo, were forced to leave the district on October 28. The two latter were discovered in the place where they had taken refuge; on October 31 they were seized by the Fascists, taken back to their own houses, and warned to quit the district within 48 hours. The ban is still in force, as the recent letter reproduced below proves. It was written by the Prefectoral Commissary of the Commune in reply to the request for a testimonial of good conduct for Toschi and Schiassi, which they needed in order to obtain work in an industrial establishment.

Molinella, 10 October, 1923.

Municipality of Molinella

N. 4275 di Prot.

Testimonial of good conduct for Toschi Marcello and Schiassi Carlo.

I regret to have to intimate to you in reply to your recent letter that I fear I cannot grant the request transmitted to me for a cerificate of good conduct for Messrs. Toschi Marcello and Schiassi Carlo.

It may be true (I am not at all sure of it) that, as you affirm, the persons in question have nothing against them, and I am even ready to believe that they are quite honest; but the political principles they profess (of which, it seems to me, you make much too light, since even liberty of thought has its limits like any other recognised liberty)—these, which are common knowledge, and also the fact that the certificate would be in regard to individuals who were driven out of their district—unjustly or not—by the rage of the people, and who were amongst those of the workpeople who were most in evidence at a time of disturbance which is not yet forgotten,—these are elements such as the head of a Communal Administration, who, above all, ought to take account of the general, common or prevailing public conviction, cannot altogether overlook.

Besides, a testimonial of good conduct from me, let me say plainly, might give grounds for speculations of a political character which it is well to avoid arousing, among other reasons in order to attain with all speed that complete pacification which is your hope and mine, and which by good fortune we have at length almost entirely succeeded in attaining.

(*Signed*) CARNEVALLI,
Prefectoral Commissary.

Following this forcible dispossession of the Co-operative and Workers' Organisations of Molinella, the Prefect of Bologna came upon the scene, not to restore them to their legitimate owners, but to sanction and legitimise their unjust expropriation with the following decrees:

(1) "Whereas, on the occasion of the disturbances towards the end of last October, the premises of the Workers' Co-operative Societies of Molinella were occupied by representatives of the National Fascist Party; and whereas, having been invited to give up the rooms of the said associations with whatever they might contain, the aforesaid representatives replied that that was their intention, and begged for an inquiry by the public authority into the working of the various bodies;

"Whereas, from expert investigations it appears that only the Agricultural Co-operative Society was regularly constituted, while, as regards the other associations, it is not possible (!) to ascertain immediately what persons legitimately represent the interests of the members, and are therefore entitled to have the respective premises restored to them;

"Whereas, under such conditions, it is clearly necessary for the moment to make provision, by means of a suitable official, for the entering into possession and for the custody of the premises and of the goods of the

Associations, reserving any other measure until the required information has been obtained by the official who will be put in charge;

"Having regard to Article 3 of the Communal and Provincial Law and the Police Law;

"The Prefect of the Province of Bologna decrees that the accountant Cavaliere Tullio Carnevalli be charged with the execution of the foregoing, with power to demand the assistance and intervention of the police. November 8, 1922."

(2) "The Prefect of the Province of Bologna, having regard to his former decree dated the 8th instant, by which the accountant Cavaliere Tullio Carnevalli was charged to arrange for entering into possession, for the purpose of custody, of the so-called Workers' Co-operative Societies of Molinella;

"Having regard to the necessity, now that the operations of handing over have been completed, of making provision for ascertaining the juridical soundness and standing of the property (!) in order to consider further measures to be adopted;

"Having regard to Article 3 of the Communal and Provincial Law and the Police Law; decrees further

"That Cavaliere Salvatore Portelli, central inspector for the Accountant-General of the Ministry of the Interior, is charged with the above-mentioned operations, assuming provisional management of the above designated property, with the exercise of the duties entailed thereby. November 13, 1922."

(3) "The Prefect of Bologna,

"Having regard to his former decrees dated the 8th and 13th of November, relative to the entering into possession of the quarters and the property of the so-called Co-operative Society of Molinella, decrees further:

"Having in view the necessity and urgency of determining the lawful ownership of the property, for manifest public reasons, in view of the way in which it came to be established, and with the object of preventing unlawful diversions and deductions of sums of money, and other applications for the benefit of third parties;

"Reserving any other measure for the suitable disposing of the aforesaid property, having in mind the legitimate interests of the receivers;

"Having regard to Article 3 of the Communal and Provincial Law and the Police Regulations;

"Decrees:

"1.   Holders of sums of money or other revenues belonging to the so-called Co-operative Society of Molinella, in all its branches of activity, accruing under whatever denomination (supply contracts, consumers' societies, machinery depôts, etc.) are hereby required to give information of the fact and to make payment to the Prefectoral Commissary charged with the provisional administration of the Co-operative Society, within five days from the date of the present order.

"2.   Debtors of these concerns are forbidden to make any payment whatever to anyone other than the Prefectoral Commissary.

"3.   The Police Authorities are charged to see to the execution of the present decree, and to the charging and prosecution of those who contravene the above provisions.   December 19, 1922."

By means of such decrees the property of all the co-operative societies, amounting to several million lire, was dispersed and sold below price to the societies' actual Fascist competitors; and persecution was begun, not of those who had appropriated the property of others, but of the lawful owners who by their work had accumulated the property.

On January 1, 1923, in the hamlet of S. Pietro Capofiume, a band of Fascists broke into the house of a workman named Mainardi Francesco, and beat him until the blood came. Another workman in the same house, Rubini Pietro, shared his fate.

On the 2nd, in the same hamlet, a Fascist band broke into the house of the farmer Frazzoni Augusto and threatened him with death because he was a member of the General Confederation of Labour.

On the 4th the foreman Schiassi Francesco, of Miravalle (a village in the Commune) was followed by a Fascist who shot at him and, coming up to him, seized him and took him to the house of the secretary of the Fascio, ordering that he should be beaten.

On the 6th, Fascists insulted and cuffed a working woman named Piazzi Lidovina in Molinella.

On the 6th two working women, named Violetta and Giuseppina Zagni, ran into the piazza of Molinella to rescue their father Zagni Attilio from Fascists who were trying to force castor oil on him. The two women were beaten.

On the 6th, in Molinella, a workman, Bianchi Gelindo, was beaten till the blood came.

On the 7th a workman, Martelli Filippo, was beaten by a Fascist.

On the 10th a workman, Cocchi Angelo, of the hamlet of Marmorta, was attacked and beaten in front of his own house by a Fascist.

On the 16th a workman, Bandiera Virgilio, of the same hamlet, was followed and shot at by a Fascist.

On the 16th a workman, Mainardi Luigi, of the same hamlet was beaten by Fascists on two occasions when he was returning from work.

* * * * *

On March 24, 1923, in the hamlet of S. Pietro Capofiume, a band of Fascists beat a workman named Selleri Alessandro in the courtyard of the house of Selleri Augusto.

On the 26th, after a meeting at the headquarters of the Fascio, two bands of Fascists formed and went off, one in the direction of the Saltarelli and Zaniboni property, and the other to the property of the heirs of Signor Spada. Their object was to secure the discharge by the farmers in the Confederation of Labour of the labourers belonging to the Confederation whom they were employing. The tenant farmer Bertoncelli and a sister of his, a war widow, were beaten; also Selleri Alessandro, Selleri Ugo, and a sister of these two, fifteen years old. This was on the Spada farm; in the Saltarelli and Zaniboni property Mazzoni Augusto, a tenant farmer, and his wife were beaten.

On the 29th, while a working woman named Gardi Caterina, of the hamlet of S. Martino, was on her way to work she was attacked by a Fascist, thrown to the ground and cuffed. In the afternoon a Fascist band visited the tenant farmers of this region, Bignami, Monti, Zucchini, Fabbri, Cirolani, Tinarelli, Grassi, Giordani, etc., all members of the Confederation of Labour, and compelled them to discharge the workers belonging to the Confederation whom they were employing, beating the son of the tenant Giordani in his own dwelling.

On the 27th a war widow, Gardi Amelia, of the hamlet of S. Martino, was arrested by carabineers, who were accompanied by the secretary of the Fascio. Her two little children were left behind; she was detained 54 days, and then released pending inquiry. She was arrested again on August 14 by the police, and detained a further 24 days, without any judicial sentence.

On April 13, in the hamlet of Marmorta, the militia and carabineers searched and arrested Vitali Antono and

Calzolari Nello, collectors of dues for the Labour Exchange.

On May 1 the workers belonging to the Confederation were suspended from work under the Reno drainage works, the only work open to them, in order to reduce them to submission through hunger.

On the 5th Fascists arrested workmen named Martelli Filippo and Rizzoli Giuseppe because they were found in possession of receipts for their payments to the Labour Exchange.

On the 15th a Fascist beat a working woman named Rubini Stella, and threatened her septuagenarian father. Fascists arrested the foreman Stagni Ettore and Fattori Giulio.

* * * * *

On August 1, 1923, while the Fascist threshing machine, imported against the will of the tenant farmer Calzolari, was threshing the corn, and the farmer's family were working in the fields, four Fascists came up to Calzolari, an old man of 70, and beat him till he bled. Returning to the farmyard, carrying their arms, they made the women and children shut themselves up in the house, and the Fascists then threshed the corn as though it had been their own property.

On the 4th a Fascist beat a workman named Mazzeri Giuseppe.

On the 5th, in Borra, in the hamlet of Marmorta, Fascists beat Colti Federico, a workman belonging to the Confederation of Labour.

On the 6th a Fascist band beat a workman named Nanni Amerigo in the hamlet of Selva, and also other workmen in the same hamlet, named Fattori Adelmo and Buriani Aldo, warning them to get out of the Confederation.

On the 9th Fascists broke into the farm tenanted by

Cocchi Luigi, where Cappellari Leonida, Zagni Erminio, Zagni Erminia, Zagni Maria and Pillani Augusto were at work. They sent them home, and when they were near the *case del popolo* they sent several revolver shots after them. Another band forced the door of the house of the widow Poggi Virginia. A band of about twenty at Borra beat workers named Baldi Mario and Zucchini Arcangelo, and also the latter's wife, who was pregnant, so that an abortion followed. Then they went to the wood of Talon, where they beat the whole family of the tenant farmer Mainardi till they bled. Finally they destroyed the roof of the house of the tenant farmer Marani Pietro, broke down the door, and killed Marani, who was an ex-service man ; his wife, seeing that he was mortally wounded, started off to fetch the doctor, but they prevented her from going.

On the 10th a band of Fascists from elsewhere attacked a workman, Mannini Sante, before the door of his own house in S. Pietro Capofiume.

On the 12th, at about 3 a.m., two bombs exploded in Molinella, one near the house of the Secretary of the Fascio, on the opposite side of the street, and the other in Malborghetto. The names of the persons who threw them were on everyone's lips, but they were not touched. At the same hour, Fascist bands from Ferrara and Bologna, who were in readiness on the borders of the Commune, entered the town and began action in grand style. A first band went to the hamlet of Selva, about nine miles off. They beat a workman named Sgargi Luigi. They seized and carried to the headquarters of the Molinella Fascio an ex-soldier named Bolognesi Giuseppe, who was interrogated, bound hands and feet, and detained for the rest of the day. Then he was taken back to his house, beaten, and shot at several times. Fifty shots were fired at a workman named Cortelli Gaetano and his son. They surrounded the house of the tenant farmer Fattori Ottario, searched it, confiscated the arms found (although he had a regular permit) and various other belongings, and beat all the members of his family who had not managed to get away. Another band of Fascists, in the hamlet of S. Pietro Capofiume, went to the Zaniboni-Saltarelli estate, where they compelled the tenants to accept as their share of the corn 50 per cent. instead of the 60 per cent. due to them under the agreement in force. They beat Presti Ezio and the whole of the Deserti family till they bled. Several bands entered the property of the Spada heirs, shooting everyone they met. The most seriously injured were the old Calzolari Paolo, who had been beaten a few days before; his son, Bertoncelli Augusto, his daughter Maínardi Settimia, a war widow, and Cazzola Isolina. The old Calzólari was taken to the hospital in Bologna, where at first he was declared to be dying. He recovered atfer several months in hospital. On the Spada estate two workmen were also beaten, Bergonzoni Gennaro (for the second time) and Montanari Roberto. Other bands went towards Marmorta, where they forced the door of the house of Bagni Gaetano, entered it, beat him for the fourth time, reducing him within an inch of death, and beat his wife and his son Giuseppe. The house of a workman, Magri Luigi, was surrounded, and he and his wife beaten. The whole of the Ariatti family were beaten. The whole of the family of Villani Luigi without distinction, men, women and children, were beaten. Two workmen, Zucchini Marcello and Cocchi Angelo, were stopped and beaten by Fascists of the locality and from elsewhere. Several shots were fired at the house of Gardi Albino, also in the hamlet of Mortara. In the hamlet of S. Martino in Argine, a workman belonging to the Confederation, Biavati Albino, was beaten by a band of six Fascists. Another band beat a workman named Giacomelli Lodovico.

At noon on this day, August 12, the Fascists published the following

"ULTIMATUM.

"The provocations of the subversive hooligans, encouraged by the anti-Fascist press of all Italy, have provoked fresh incidents and fresh conflicts.

"The Fascist organisations of Molinella invite all the young men who have come in from every part of the Province of Bologna to return without delay to their own villages, and invite the Red farmers and workers to desist from an unjustified and criminal resistance.

"A forty-eight hours' truce is granted to the organised members who still adhere to the Socialist League, to enable them to declare their submission; after this period the struggle will be resumed in full force until an end has been put to a situation which is being taken advantage of in Italy and abroad, and which is a dishonour to Molinella. It is the desire and the duty of Molinella to be quickly and completely won over to the Nation.

"THE FASCIST GROUP.

"Molinella, August 12, 1923."

August 13, 1923. "I, the undersigned Galbiani Alberta, was on my way home at 7 p.m. on August 13, after reaping flax, when at Case Nuove the Fascists . . . caught hold of me and took me to the Fascio, where I was detained until the morning of the 15th, and then released, after having been continually threatened with a revolver placed close to my head. . . . One of the brothers . . . threatened me with a rope, with which he said he would bind me hand and foot and hang me. Then six Fascists of Mezzolara wanted to give me a whole dose of chloroform to make me unconscious. . . . compelled me to sign membership of the Fascist trade union or to stop still longer in their hands. On the morning of the 14th I saw them bring in front of me my husband, Mingozzi Francesco, whom they had been to fetch from home, where he was lying ill in bed. In front of me they bound him hand and foot to a chair for some hours of the day, and . . . threatened that if he did not comply with his demands they would cut him to pieces. He, too, was released on the 15th after being compelled to sign membership of the National trade union or remain still in their hands. All day and night . . . Fascists of the village and other places did nothing but spit at me; they insulted me worse than a woman of the streets.

(Signed) GALBIANI ALBERTINA."

August 14. The mass of the farmers and labourers, rather than join the Fascist trade union, left the Commune. Then the Fascists closed the boundaries and prevented anyone from passing out. Fascist bands visited the women in their homes, made them sign membership of the Fascist trade union, and gave them passes to go out of the Commune if they promised to go in search of their husbands and to make them sign too.

Fasci Italiani di Combattimento.

Molinella Section.

The women named below . . . . are proceeding to Bologna to communicate to their husbands the "ultimatum" received from this Fascio, promising to induce them to submit.

(Stamp of the National Fascist Party,
Molinella Section.)

Molinella, August 12, 1923.

Fasci Italiani di Combattimento.
Molinella Section.

Signora . . . is proceeding to Bologna for service reasons.

(*Signed*) LUIGI BILLI.

(*Stamp of the National Fascist Party, Molinella Section.*)

August 14. Carabineers and Fascist militiamen arrested and detained in prison for a week the workpeople Rubini Rosa, Neri Cleta, Cazzola Albina, Chiavelli Alberto, Neri Romeo, Pancaldi Angelo, without any legal proceedings ensuing.

August 14. Carabineers and Fascist militiamen arrested and detained in prison for a fortnight 35 men and 11 women, without any legal proceedings ensuing.

August 14. Fascists and carabineers proceeded to the home of Fornasini Cesare. Finding no one there, they returned on the night of the 15th, forced the door, and made a search; repeating the procedure nightly until the 18th.

August 14. A workman named Poli Gaetano was arrested and taken to Molinella gaol in a motor lorry, and beaten on the way. Another workman, Draghetti Roberto, suffered the same fate. The family of a third, Rubini Pompeo, were beaten.

August 14. In the hamlet of S. Martino the wife of Maiani Carlo was arrested; in the same hamlet a workman named Chiarini Cesare was beaten.

August 15. A workman named Bondi Riccardo was taken to the premises of the Fascio and beaten. Garuti Natalina, an old woman 76 years of age, was taken to the Fascio at 2 a.m. and released at 4 a.m. In the hamlet of Selva, Fascists arrested the tenant farmer Fattori Ettore, and in the hamlet of Marmorta the farmer Cavallini Enea, who was afterwards released, and then re-arrested and beaten many times out of doors and in barracks.

August 15. Twenty men and eight women were arrested by carabineers and Fascist militiamen and kept a fortnight in gaol because they refused to join Fascist trade unions. No legal action ensued.

August 15. Nine men and a woman were beaten and arrested by carabineers and Fascist militiamen, and detained a fortnight in gaol.

August 15. Carabineers and Fascist militiamen made nocturnal searches in the house of a workman named Tinarelli Fioravante, and tried to induce him to join the Fascist union. Fascists forced the lock of the house of Stagni Luigi, and entered the house. Fascists and carabineers proceeded to the house of a workman named Reggiani and enjoined him to sign membership of the Fascist union, on pain of arrest and beating if he refused. Four men and two women in the hamlet of Selva were arrested and detained for a fortnight.

August 16. In the hamlet of Marmorta, Fascists arrested and cuffed a working woman named Bagni Carmela, who, together with another named Musiani Farnanda, was detained under arrest for a fortnight. In the hamlet of S. Martino in Argine a workman named Falzoni Fernando, who had already been beaten on July 16, was arrested, insulted and ill-treated. In the hamlet of Selva two working women, Pagani Giuseppina, a war widow, and Barbieri Adalgisa, were arrested. A workman named Cortelli Leonida was arrested at Bologna because he refused to sign membership of the Fascist trade union.

August 17. In the hamlet of S. Martino in Argine, Bentivogli Giuseppe, an old man of 79, was arrested. In the hamlet of Marmorta the house of a workman named Calzolari Alfredo was searched and his clothes and bicycle seized.

August 23.. A Fascist band in Marmorta, carrying revolvers, entered the house of the Bevilacqua family, threatened the whole household, and seized a sporting gun. Bevilacqua was arrested in the hamlet by carabineers and Fascist militiamen. He was detained some hours, and then released. On his arrival at home he was pursued again by Fascists. Scenting what was in preparation, he jumped out of the window, and was shot at. In the hamlet of Selva Malvezzi, a workman named Callegari Ettore was arrested and detained until the 27th.

December. The Socialist daily, *Giustizia* ("Justice") published a subscription list containing some thousands of names of men and women workers of Molinella in honour of Filippo Turati.

On the same morning the brigadier of carabineers of Marmorta searched the house of Villani Luigi, who had been indicated as the collector of the subscriptions.

The big farmers loaded up lorries with workers from the hamlets and took them to Molinella on the pretext of a trade union meeting. At the meeting the subscription list was read over, and the subscribers present were held prisoners and 28 of them made to sign a telegram of protest against the subscription.

In the evening a band of local and Ferrarese Fascists, armed with rifles and revolvers, entered the house of Villani Luigi, and beat a workman named Machelli Mario, whom they found there, until the blood came. The brothers Virgilio and Augusto Badiera and their old mother were also ferociously beaten.

A workman named Musiari Isidoro and his brother were brought almost to the point of death.

As a consequence of this same subscription for *Giustizia,* Fascists penetrated into the house of Cenacchi Giuseppe in the hamlet of S. Martino in Argine, and beat him until the blood came, and his son

Manlio and daughter Margherita with him; further, a workman named Ghelli Nello, his old mother, and his sister Angelina. Stagni Ettore, ex-non-commissioned officer at the front, was attacked in his own house and beaten until the blood came, in the presence of his five weeping children. A workman named Sassatelli Anello was attacked in his own house and beaten, and after jumping out of the window he was fired at from rifles and revolvers. In the hamlet of S. Pietro Capofiume a band of Fascists beat Mainardi Stefano and Mainardi Francesco; and a workman named Lanzoni Antonio was beaten in his own house.

Meanwhile the police proceeded to the arrest—of those who had been beaten, and of a further twenty workers guilty of having subscribed to *Giustizia;* some of them were kept in prison for several days.

The acts of violence detailed above were endured by the organised masses of the Commune without any single one of them retorting in kind, in accordance with the resolution passed by the general meeting in March, 1922. On the other hand, not one day's imprisonment was imposed on those responsible for the outrages, although every one was reported to the police.

PART VI.

THE FREEDOM OF THE PRESS.

December 6, 1922. "No progress can be made like this. Fascist circles nearest to the Government are determined to impose discipline on the newspapers as well. . . . In face of the spectacle daily offered by certain journals, no one will be surprised if the Fascist Government imposes a censorship and adopts still severer measures." *Popolo d'Italia* (Mussolini's paper).

December 7. "To all those concerned : a warning for their good. If it is the case that the Socialist papers, and in particular the so-called 'Unitary' *Giustizia,* have abandoned themselves to the most Jesuitical campaigns against the Government . . .

"It is time to ask these gentlemen to stop it. The Fascist revolution has been generous. . . . But woe to the Socialist and Communist leaders if they take undue advantage of it. The Fascist revolution has not proceeded to summary executions—and might very well have done so. But mind where you are going, old rabble of Italian Socialism." *Popolo d'Italia* (Mussolini's paper).

December 13. "The Executive of the *Fascio di Combattimento* (Militant Fascists) of Milan . . . warns the editorial board of the journal *La Giustizia* not to give publicity any longer to statements which are devoid of any foundation in fact, or tendencious, or such as to excite class hatred, and gives notice that, should it continue to practise this perverse type of journalism, the Milan *Fascio* will decide on the measures which it deems necessary to restore it to the observance of proper standards of journalistic correctness and honesty." *Popolo d'Italia* (Mussolini's paper).

January 5, 1923. The police authorities send a circular to the newspapers, to "intimate, by Government order, that they must not publish any news of the mutiny of the *Guardia Regia* at Naples, Turin, Rome, and elsewhere, except such as is circulated by the Government itself—under penalty of such 'sanctions' as the Government shall apply . . . *in virtue of its plenary powers*" (!?)

March 6. "The '*Corriere* is uneasy' ! For any pates that may be raised there are five hundred thousand bludgeons always ready. And there are people ready for anything. And there is a Fascist militia. And, if need be, there will be good machine-guns and hand-grenades. Let the *Corriere* then sleep soundly. . . . And leave it to the Fascist State !" *Popolo d'Italia.*

April 6. "The patience of the leaders of Fascism has been enormous and perhaps excessive; it cannot be allowed to go on being abused with impunity. Woe to those who are abusing it if the Fascist leaders are compelled, in the face of these foul insults, to utter the terrible historical cry, 'A noi !'[1] A word to the wise. Not before it is time !" *Popolo d'Italia.*

* * * * *

June 24. "The best reply would be the sacred cudgel which has so often punished League leaders, guilty more than any of . . . drunkenness and ignorance, and which has in no case brought injury to the nation. These scribes, on the other hand, damage the nation in the face of the foreigner, and there is unfortunately no means of silencing them unless once for all the necessary limitation of the freedom of the press is put into effect. . . .

"As for the Fascist bludgeon, nobody says that it should not and may not be called into use at any moment." *Popolo d'Italia* (dealing with an article by Prof. Guglielmo Ferrero, in the *Secolo*).

July 8. "Senator Albertini (i.e., *Corriere della Sera*), Listen to us ! Senator Albertini, we have been putting

[1] i.e., "Up, and at them !"

up with you for a long time, far too long, and we tell you plainly that we have had enough of it ! . . . Senator Albertini, there are so many Fascists—so many ! so many ! so many !—known, very well known, and unknown, in many towns of Italy, who write to us asking nothing more than to share all the honour and the dignity of being present at the razing to the ground of your miserable 'shanty.' [1] If that has not yet happened, you can well imagine whom you have to thank, Senator Albertini ! But give it up, I beg you. And I beg this from no love of you or of your paper."
Popolo d'Italia.

July 8. "The slippery Liberal Senator,[2] morally responsible for the assassinations of Fascists which have lately been perpetrated by the red rabble whose open and cynical ally he now is, is trying to shuffle and quibble. We shall not allow it. It is time to ram down his throat the cry of 'Liberty for ever !' because this intriguer has full liberty to spit upon the Government, has in fact liberty to poke fun at the gesture of the Government when it fell on its knees on the 4th November [3] . . . Does Senator Albertini then admit in full his complicity with the Communists ? . . . When it appears, as is and can be proved, that the Leninists of Moscow quote the *Corriere's* articles and count on the Liberal Senator Albertini's anti-Fascist campaign, the red brand which marks him with blood is definite and ineffaceable. Let the Fascists remember !" *Popolo d'Italia.*

July 11. "Signor Mussolini declares that last November he prepared regulations against abuses on the part of the Press, but that he has kept on postponing

[1] The Milan offices of the *Corriere della Sera* are of great magnificence.—*Trans.*
[2] Albertini.—*Trans.*
[3] The anniversary of the Austrian capitulation.—*Trans.*

their issue in the hope of things improving.[1] With the disappearance of the danger of illegal direct action on the part of Fascism, its opponents have raised their heads again and are pursuing an intensified campaign of subornation. . . . The Fascist Government is bound to intervene, either in prevention or in swift punishment. . . . The Council unanimously delegates to three Ministers the task of proposing the measures to be adopted.'' *Council of Ministers* (official communiqué).

July 12. "The Council of Ministers has approved the decree concerning the press, under which the Prefect of the Province is authorised to warn and in due course to suspend a newspaper which by means of false or tendencious statements embarrasses the diplomatic action of the Government, or damages the national credit at home or abroad, or raises an unjustified alarm among the population, or in any manner whatever disturbs public order; . . . if it incites to hatred or disobedience to the law, or disturbs the discipline of those employed in a public service . . ." *Council of Ministers* (official communiqué).

July 16. "H.M. the King has signed the decree concerning new press regulations. The decree is therefore in the hands of the Prime Minister, who will use his discretion as to issuing it at an opportune moment." *Official communiqué.*

November, 1922 (*Genoa*). The daily *Il Lavoro* ("Labour") only allowed to resume publication on condition of discharging its editor, the Deputy Canepa, and its news editor, Signor Ansaldo.

November 27, *Portoferraio* (*Leghorn*). Fascists attack a Catholic named Imparato, one of the staff of the journal *La Difesa* ("Defence").

[1] These regulations were at length issued by Signor Mussolini when things had so improved that the author of this pamphlet had been murdered.—*Trans.*

November 24 (*Florence*). The Fascists start a policy of intimidating newsvendors in order to induce them to give up the sale of publications which are "subversive" or considered as such. They propose that the newsvendors shall exhibit a placard to this effect.

December 20 (*Naples*). Fascists invade and sack the premises of the journal *Le Battaglie del Mezzogiorno* ("Noonday Battles"). The editor protests against 4,000 lire being taken; the Fascists deny the theft and complete the sack of the building.

At midnight the Fascists invade and sack the premises of *Il Giorno* ("Day"), Matilde Serao'ṡ daily.

Locate Triulzi (*Milan*). Fascists from Legnano appear at the Post Office, and seize 450 copies of the Socialist paper *La Difesa* ("Defence").

December 8 (*Ravenna*). Fascists invade and destroy the printing-room of the paper *La Romagna Socialista* ("Socialist Romagna"), and beat the printer for expressing disapproval.

Melfi (*Potenza*). Fascists prevent the issue of the Socialist paper *Il Lavoratore* ("The Worker").

December 10 (*Novara*). Fascists wreck the printing-room of the *Parola Socialista* ("Socialist Word"), and carry off the printing plant.

December 30 (*Florence*). A newsvendor named Narciso Clari ordered, because he did not "cry" the *Popolo d'Italia,* to drink a glass full of castor oil. When he curtly refuses he is cudgelled.

March 13, 1923 (*Molinella*). The journalists, Mr. and Mrs. Waterfield, of the *Times,* surrounded in a house, taken to the Fascist headquarters, and not released for some time.

March 22 (*Florence*). A Socialist tramwayman named Torquato Gineprai, who was collecting funds for his party's paper, cudgelled by the Fascists. Two tramwaymen, Belliconi and Bacci, dragged to the Fascist headquarters, warned and threatened.

* * * * *

June 6 (*Naples*). A Fascist band breaks into the house of Carlo Epifani, the editor of a paper friendly to the Fascists; they smash everything and beat Signor Epifani until the blood runs, on account of an article of his.

June 6 (*Cremona*). Fascists make a second attempt to invade the premises of the journal *La Provincia,* and to break down the entrance gate.

" . . . For my part, every time that the Democratic journal *La Provincia,* or any other paper of that firm's, disparages the Fascism of Cremona . . . I shall amuse myself by clouting the editor or someone for it. This is not lack of discipline; it is permissible for anyone, for the good of the party and the nation, to attack a few old buffers, or the rotten decision of a magistrate." *Farinacci* (leader of the Cremona Fascists).

July 7 (*Biella*). A prefect's decree suspends the *Corriere Biellese* for an article criticising the Government.

July 3 (*Trieste*). Fascists march on the premises of the *Lavoratore* ("Worker"), throwing bombs and firing revolvers.

July 4 (*Bergamo*). The chief reporter of the newspaper *Eco di Bergamo* ("Bergamo Echo") beaten by Fascists for his account of a local affair.

July 13 (*Monza*). At night several lorries full of armed Fascists penetrate into the Palazzo Raiberti and wreck the printing-room of the newspaper *Il Cittadino* ("The Citizen"). Damage : 300,000 lire.

Treviso. The Prefect suspends the publication of the Republican paper *La Riscossa* ("Insurrection"). The copies of the paper seized and the editorial and administrative offices searched.

July 14 (*Ancona*). Fascists seize the papers *Corriere della Sera, Popolo,* and *Voce Repubblicana* and burn them in the middle of the piazza.

June 16 (*Viareggio*). Fascists beat the editor of the weekly *Gazzetta della Riviera,* because he is a candidate for Parliament, and seize the paper.

July 17 (*Milan*). The editorial offices of *L'Italia* burnt by bombs being thrown into them.

July 18 (*Lucera*). The *Popolo di Capitanata* ("The People of C.") suspends publication in order to avoid "a free voice being suffocated by violent means."

July 19 (*Monza*). Fascists make the proprietor of the newspaper stall hand over to them the copies of the *Sindacato Rosso* ("Red Trade Union"), and destroy them in the piazza.

July 22 (*Biella*). The lawyer David Nissim, chairman of the Liberals; the accountant Dante Coda, editor of the *Tribuna Biellese*; and Enrico Sarri, attacked and beaten by Fascists, on account of an article published in that paper.

* * * * *

October 27 (*Civitavecchia*). Fascists prevent the sale of the *Voce Repubblicana,* and make away with the bundles of papers.

October 29 (*Florence*). A newsvendor named Secondo Giorni dragged to the Fascist headquarters, threatened with serious violence,—an imitation pyre being set alight,—and warned not to sell "subversive" papers any longer.

October 26 (*Florence*). A newsvendor named Ronchi cudgelled by Fascists for distributing "subversive" publications.

November 15 (*Forli*). In the Piazza Saffi, Fascists beat a Republican student named Baldi Eraldo till the blood runs. The copies of the *Pensiero Romagnolo* ("Romagna Opinion") in the newsvendors' stalls seized and burnt in the piazza.

November 29 (*Padua*). The premises of the Republican Party searched, and circulars about the distribution of the *Voce Repubblicana* seized.

November 29. The police search the editorial office of the Republican review *Humanitas,* and seize registers and letters.

November 4, 1923. " . . The reader will think that it is a question of some Greek daily paper. No, sir! The only Greek is the author of the article; the paper, which calls itself Italian, is published in Italy, in fact at Naples: we refer, in fact, to the *Giorno* ("Day"), which is disgusting even at night!

"And it will continue to be as long as the Neapolitan Fascists allow it. . . ." *Popolo d'Italia* (Mussolini's paper).

November 28. "It is excusable that the Italians, who have made a revolution in order to renovate Italy, should sometimes itch to throw their boots at the old distorting mirror (*Corriere della Sera*) in order to enjoy the pleasure of hearing the crash of the fragments.

"Let the *Corriere* continue under the guidance of its 'objectivity,' obscured by a pair of smoked spectacles, if it chooses. Let it remember, however, that that is the best way to pay cash down for trouble." *Popolo d'Italia* (Mussolini's paper).

The daily *Giustizia,* the organ of the Unitary Socialist Party, is constantly the victim of Fascist violence. Apart from the districts into which, even by 1922, the paper could not penetrate at all, we mention some new ones added in the year of Fascism:

Cagli (*Pesaro*). On December 7 the copies which the vendor had received were burned, and he was given an injunction to refuse the paper.

Carmagnola (*Turin*). Fascist pressure hinders the sale of the paper, and on that account the management has to suspend despatch.

Casale Monferrato (Alessandria). Sale prohibited.

Castellamonte (Turin). Sale prohibited.

Cavarzere (Venice). On February 7 Fascists prevent the sale of the paper. In consequence, the despatch of copies is suspended.

Chiaravalle (Ancona). Sale prevented from September 5, 1922.

Variago (Emilia). Fascists prevent the sale of the paper by threats.

Abbiategrasso (Milan). On November 6 Fascists seize the copies on arrival, and enjoin the vendors not to accept the paper any more.

Alessandria. Fascists burn a newspaper stall because the "subversive" papers, including the *Giustizia,* are sold there.

And so at *Ancona, Bitonto (Bari), Cittadella, Collecchio (Parma), Corato (Bari), Fano (Pesaro), Firenzuola d'Adda (Parma), Ficarolo (Rovigo), Iglesias, Lovere (Bergamo), Marciano Marina (Leghorn), Metelica (Macerata), Montemarciano (Ancona), Ponte dell' Oglio (Cremona), Pontedera (Pisa), Porto-civitanova (Macerata), Portogruaro (Venice), Porto-maggiore (Ferrara), Porto S. Giorgio (Ascoli Piceno), Rimini, Settimo Torinese, Solferino (Mantua), Valenza (Alessandria), Molinella,* and so on.

December 10, 1923 *(Milan).* At night, after a speech of the Fascist Minister Giuriati, against the Opposition Parties, *La Giustizia,* the Unitary Socialist Party's daily, is attacked by Fascists and its offices wrecked.